MATH MADE EASY

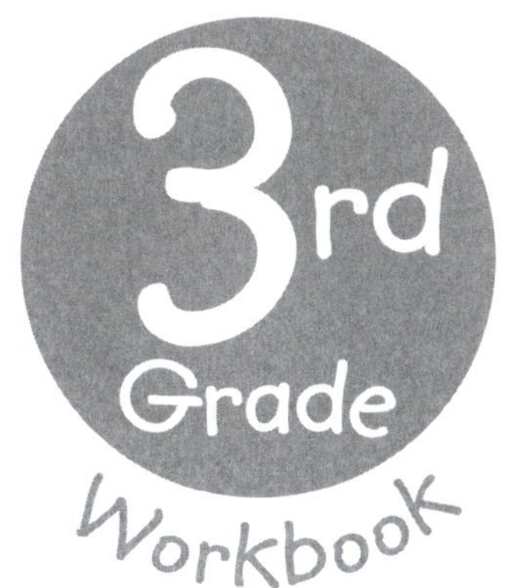

10 Minutes A Day Problem Solving

Authors

Sean McArdle and Darius McArdle

Consultant

Alison Tribley

10-minute challenge

Try to complete the exercises for each topic in 10 minutes or less. Note the time it takes you in the "Time taken" column below.

DK London
Editors Elizabeth Blakemore, Jolyon Goddard
Senior Editor Deborah Lock
US Editor Allison Singer
US Math Consultant Alison Tribley
Managing Editor Christine Stroyan
Managing Art Editor Anna Hall
Senior Production Editor Andy Hilliard
Senior Production Controller Jude Crozier
Jacket Design Development Manager Sophia MTT
Publisher Andrew Macintyre
Associate Publishing Director Liz Wheeler
Art Director Karen Self
Publishing Director Jonathan Metcalf

DK Delhi
Senior Editor Rupa Rao
Senior Art Editor Stuti Tiwari Bhatia
Editorial Team Manjari Thakur, Nishtha Kapil
Art Editor Dheeraj Arora
Managing Editors Soma B. Chowdhury, Kingshuk Goshal
Managing Art Editors Ahlawat Gunjan, Govind Mittal
Senior DTP Designer Tarun Sharma
DTP Designers Anita Yadav, Rakesh Kumar, Harish Aggarwal
Senior Jacket Designer Suhita Dharamjit
Jackets Editorial Coordinator Priyanka Sharma

This American Edition, 2020
First American Edition, 2015
Published in the United States by DK Publishing
1450 Broadway, Suite 801, New York, NY 10018

20 21 22 23 24 10 9 8 7 6 5 4 3 2 1
001–322750–May/2020

Published in Great Britain by Dorling Kindersley Limited

A catalog record for this book is available from the Library of Congress.
ISBN 978-0-7440-3153-9

DK books are available at special discounts when purchased in bulk for sales promotions, premiums, fund-raising, or educational use. For details, contact: DK Publishing Special Markets, 1450 Broadway, Suite 801, New York, NY 10018
SpecialSales@dk.com

Printed and bound in Canada

For the curious

www.dk.com

Contents

Time Taken

Time Filler:
In these boxes are some extra challenges to extend your skills. You can do them if you have some time left after finishing the questions. Or, these can be stand-alone activities that you can do in 10 minutes.

Seconds, Minutes, and Hours

Knowing your times tables well will help you convert between seconds, minutes, and hours.

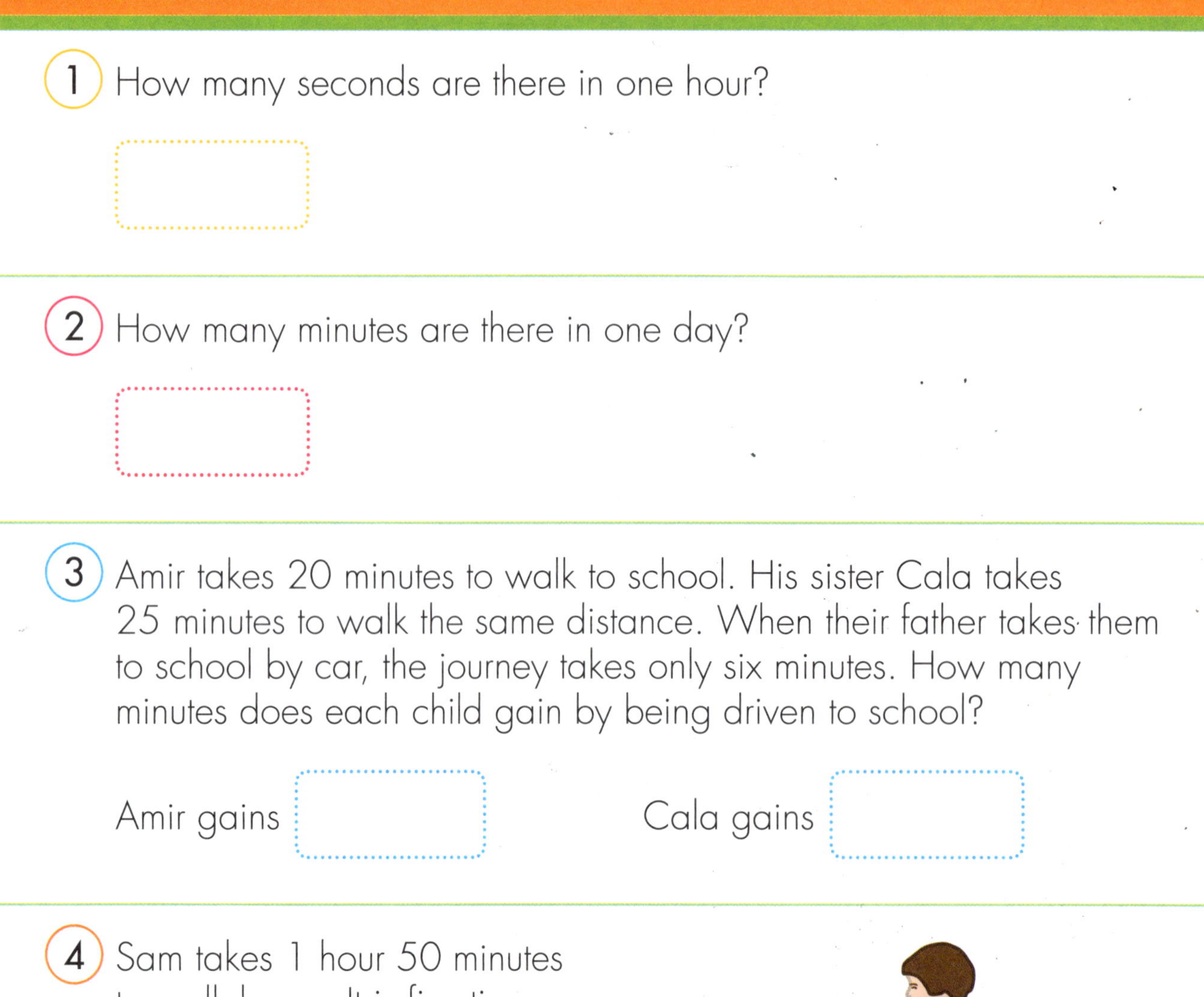

1. How many seconds are there in one hour?

2. How many minutes are there in one day?

3. Amir takes 20 minutes to walk to school. His sister Cala takes 25 minutes to walk the same distance. When their father takes them to school by car, the journey takes only six minutes. How many minutes does each child gain by being driven to school?

   Amir gains

   Cala gains

4. Sam takes 1 hour 50 minutes to walk home. It is five times quicker for him if he takes a bus home. How long does it take Sam to get home by bus?

Time Filler:
Can you figure out how much time you spend each day watching TV, doing homework, and eating? First write the time in hours and minutes, and then just in minutes. On which activity do you spend the most time each day?

5) Add together the number of minutes in one hour, three-quarters of an hour, half an hour, and a quarter of an hour.

6) Terry likes his eggs to be boiled for 270 seconds. How long is that in minutes and seconds?

7) Henry and Francine used a timer to record the time it took them to beat a computer game. Henry beat the game in 2 minutes 38 seconds, and Francine beat the game in 1 minute 42 seconds. How much quicker is Francine than Henry?

8) It took Dani 3 hours 45 minutes to complete the first ten levels of a new video game. Alex, however, completed them in only 55 minutes. How much quicker was Alex than Dani?

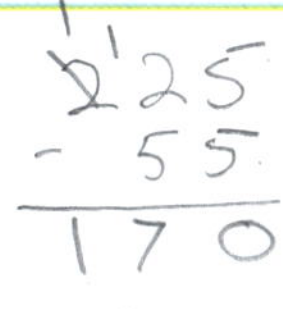

Days, Weeks, and Months

Converting quickly between days and weeks will help you practice your seven times table.

1) Daisy's grandmother gives her 50 ¢ every week. If Daisy has collected $4 from her grandmother without spending any money, for how many months has she been getting money from her grandmother? (Assume 1 month = 4 weeks)

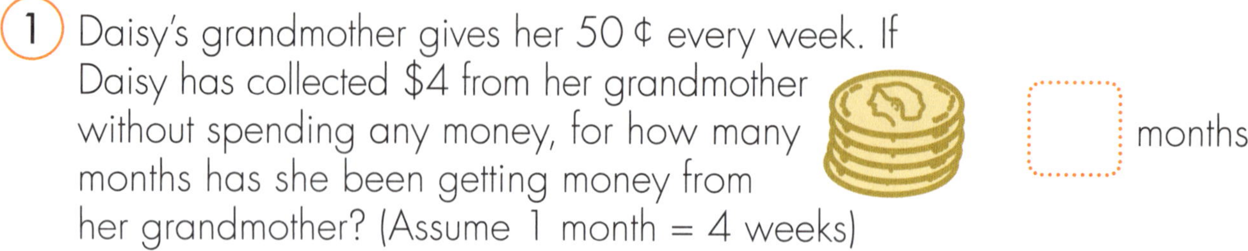

☐ months

2) It takes Mario and his parents four days to drive to a beach resort. They stay at the resort for 11 days and return home by a different route, which takes them only two days. How long is the whole trip in weeks and days?

☐ weeks ☐ days

3) Brad wants to travel the world. He begins by spending 12 weeks in Poland. He then spends 24 weeks in the United Kingdom, eight weeks in Australia, and 12 weeks in China. Lastly, he spends four weeks in South Africa before returning home. How long does Brad spend traveling? Write the answer in months. (Assume 1 month = 4 weeks)

☐ months

4) Add together the number of days in the months of May, June, and July.

☐ days

Time Filler:
Write down the birthdays of your family members. Can you figure out the gaps between the dates in:
- months, weeks, and days?
- weeks and days?
- days?

5 List the months that have 30 days, the months that have 31 days, and the month that has either 28 or 29 days.

Months with 30 days ....

Months with 31 days ....

Month with 28 or 29 days ....

6 Bella has a test coming up in four weeks. She decides to study five days each week and take the remaining days of the week off. How many days in total will Bella spend studying for the test?

☐ days

7 How many months are there in 12 years?

☐ months

8 A sailor has been on a ship for 60 days. How many weeks and days is that?

☐ weeks ☐ days

Years, Decades, and Centuries

How quickly and accurately can you answer these questions?

1 A crack in a wall lengthens by 1 in each year. If the crack is 3 in long now, how long will it be after…

1 year? ________ 1 decade? ________

2 Jacob was born in 2004.

How old will Jacob be in the year 2017? ________ years

Will Jacob be 50 in the 2040s, 2050s, or 2060s? ________

3 Here is a list of some famous events in American history. Look at the years in which they happened. Write the year a century before and a century after each event.

Event	Year	Century Before	Century After
Louisiana Purchase	1803	....	....
Beginning of the Civil War	1861	....	....
Apollo 11 moon landing	1969	....	....

Time Filler:
Find out the years in which your grandparents and parents were born. Can you determine how much older than you they are in:
- decades and years?
- years?

4 What is the year a decade before each of these years?

2008 1990 2003

5 What is the year a decade after each of these years?

1972 1995 2015

6 What is the year a century before each of these years?

1918 1999 2015

7 What is the year a century after each of these years?

980 1999 1968

8 What name do we give to a period of 1,000 years? ....

Time Problems 1

Do you have the time
to solve these problems?

1. Mary's mother wants a meal to be ready at 5:30 PM. It will take 45 minutes for the meal to cook. At what time should Mary's mother put the meal in the oven?

2. A movie begins at 7:30 PM and is 2 hours 35 minutes long. At what time will the movie end?

3. Lunchtime begins at 12:30 PM and ends at 1:10 PM. How long is lunchtime?

4. Jay is planning a road trip to visit his friend Amanda for her birthday. It will take Jay 3 hours to drive from his house to Amanda's house. The times listed below are the times Jay may choose to start his trip. For each, write the time that Jay will arrive at Amanda's.

9:15 AM

10:05 AM

4:20 PM

5:10 PM

Time Filler:
Make a list of all the different devices in your home that show the time. How many can you find? Which room in your home has the most time-telling devices?

5 A soccer match begins at 2:00 PM and lasts for 1 hour 47 minutes. At what time does the match end?

6 Write the following times using numerals.

Five hours before noon

Five hours after noon

7 How many minutes are between 11:10 PM and 12:05 AM?

8 Pam and Zoe have a ballet class at 3:20 PM and spend 1 hour 10 minutes there. At what time does the class end?

Time Problems 2

Remember to be careful when changing between units of time.

1 Two teachers recorded the time taken by children in a race. One teacher recorded the time in minutes and seconds, but the other recorded it in seconds. The table below shows the results.

Name	Time Taken
Stuart	2 minutes 5 seconds
Li	120 seconds
Mona	172 seconds
Zane	1 minute 55 seconds

Based on these results, who won the race?

How much longer did Stuart take than Li?

2 Sophie and Jake have to travel from New York to Philadelphia. The journey will take 2 hours 10 minutes. If Sophie and Jake leave New York at 11:35 AM, what time will they arrive in Philadelphia?

3 What is 50 hours in days and hours?

4 A snail takes eight hours to travel 1 m. How long will the snail take to travel 3 m?

Time Filler:
Can you figure out how many seconds there are in a week? You can check your work using a calculator.

5 A train left Silver Spring at 10:03. Before reaching Bethesda, the train waited at a signal for eight minutes. It arrived at Bethesda at 11:05. If the train had not stopped at the signal, how long would the journey have taken?

6 How many hours is the same as 300 minutes?

7 Which is longer: 170 seconds or 2 minutes 40 seconds?

8 Darius has a 10-week vacation between graduating high school and going to college. His vacation begins the first week of July.

In which month will his vacation end? ....

In which month will he be halfway through his vacation? ....

Money Problems 1

Knowing how to solve problems about money is a very important skill. Read each problem carefully.

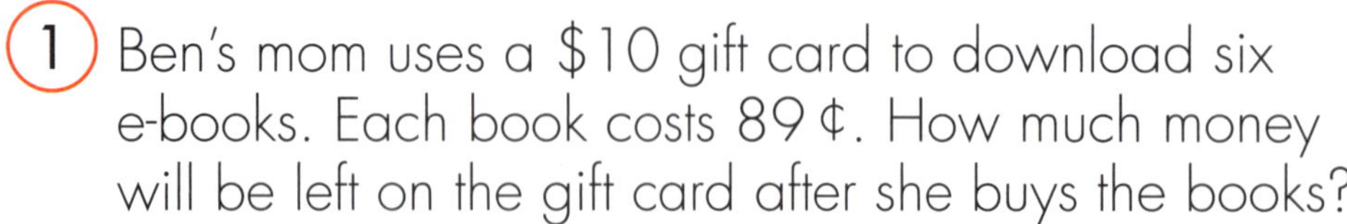

1. Ben's mom uses a $10 gift card to download six e-books. Each book costs 89 ¢. How much money will be left on the gift card after she buys the books?

2. Kelly plays an online game that costs her 40 ¢ per hour. If she plays the game for 29 hours in a year, how much will it cost her?

3. Emmie likes a winter coat she saw at a store for $67.99. She will get a discount of $12.50 if she buys the coat online. How much will the coat cost online?

4. Half of an amount is 85 ¢. How much is the whole amount?

5. A magazine costs $3.50. During a special sale, it was sold at half its price. For how much was the magazine sold?

Time Filler:
Using a maximum of ten coins, come up with different ways to make a total of $1. One way, for example, is four quarters.

6 How much is 35¢ less than $5?

7 A one-way train ticket costs $3.60. A round-trip ticket for the same journey costs $4.20. If a lady buys two one-way tickets instead of a round-trip ticket, how much extra will the tickets cost her?

8 Fran and Joseph went to a carnival together. They spent $2 on tickets, $1.60 on balloons, 70¢ on cotton candy, and 80¢ on masks. If they started with a total amount of $10 between them, how much money do they have left?

9 Danny was given $20. He saved a quarter of the money for himself and used the rest to treat his friends to dinner. How much money did Danny spend on dinner?

Length Problems 1

When measuring length, it is important to know all of the units and their abbreviations.

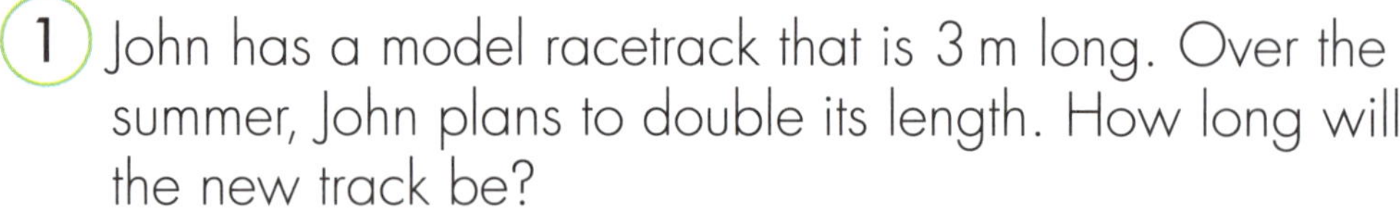

1. John has a model racetrack that is 3 m long. Over the summer, John plans to double its length. How long will the new track be?

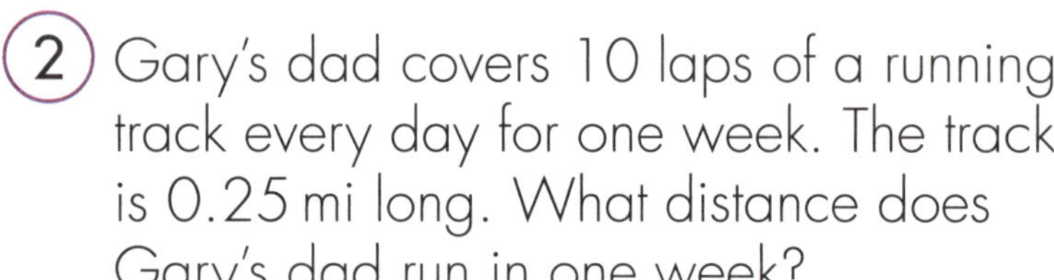

2. Gary's dad covers 10 laps of a running track every day for one week. The track is 0.25 mi long. What distance does Gary's dad run in one week?

3. Add 25 meters to each of the following lengths.

2.5 m   3.1 m   0.75 m

4. One foot is equal to 12 in. How many inches are in three feet?

Time Filler:
Measure the height of each person in your family in inches. Can you figure out the differences between each of their heights?

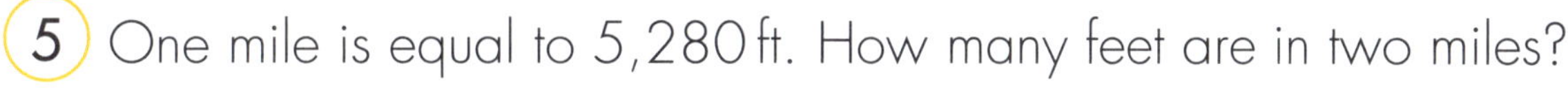

5 One mile is equal to 5,280 ft. How many feet are in two miles?

6 Add these lengths and write the answer in inches.

2.5 in + 1 ft + 3.5 in

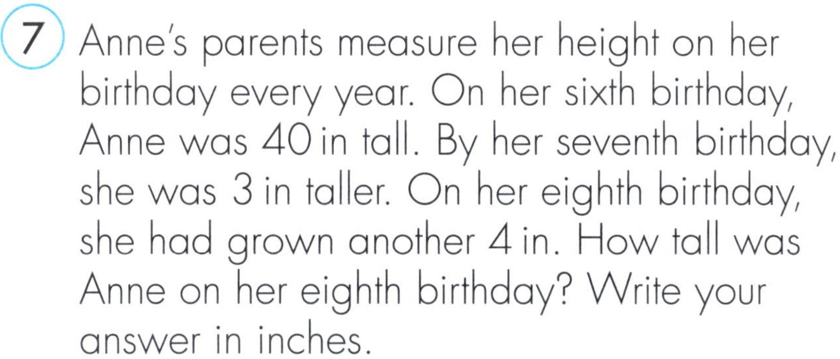

7 Anne's parents measure her height on her birthday every year. On her sixth birthday, Anne was 40 in tall. By her seventh birthday, she was 3 in taller. On her eighth birthday, she had grown another 4 in. How tall was Anne on her eighth birthday? Write your answer in inches.

8 Write these distances in feet.

6 yd

72 in

114 in

Length Problems 2

Here is some more practice in measuring lengths and changing between units.

1. A garden hedge that is 26 ft long is being trimmed. Half of the hedge has already been trimmed. What length remains?

2. Sean traveled from Beverly Hills to San Marcos in three stages. He first traveled from Beverly Hills to Santa Ana, which is a distance of 42 mi. From Santa Ana, he traveled 17 mi to Mission Viejo. Finally, he traveled a distance of 51 mi from Mission Viejo to San Marcos. How far did Sean travel in total?

3. Barbara thinks 42 m multiplied by six is 251 m. But she is incorrect.

   What is the correct answer?

   By how much is Barbara wrong?

4. How many inches are equal to 12 ft?

Time Filler:
Use the Internet or a map to find out the distances in miles between some of your favorite places. Make a list of the distances, from the shortest to the longest.

5) Two lengths added together make a total of 6 ft. If one length is 40 in, what is the other? Write your answer in inches.

6) Joel took 10 minutes to walk 800 m. If he covered the entire distance at a consistent speed, how far did Joel walk in one minute?

7) A penny has a diameter of 19 mm. If eight pennies are laid out in a straight line, what will be the length of this line?

8) A cow grazes a distance of 2 mi each day. How far will the cow have grazed in one week?

Perimeter Problems

Remember to include the measurement units—such as inches (in), feet (ft), centimeters (cm), and meters (m)—when writing distances.

1. The perimeter of a square is 64 in. What is the length of each side?

2. The perimeter of a rectangle is 36 in. If the length of the rectangle is 12 in, find its width.

3. The width of a rectangle is half its length. If the perimeter is 18 in, what are the rectangle's length and width?

   Length Width

4. Emma plays basketball on a court that is 100 ft long and 49 ft wide. To warm up before a game, Emma ran once around the perimeter of the court. How far did Emma run?

Time Filler:
Estimate in inches the perimeter of a few rectangular objects, such as TV or computer screens and books. Write down your estimates. Then use a ruler to measure the objects. How close were your estimates?

5 Look at the dimensions of the rectangle and find its perimeter.

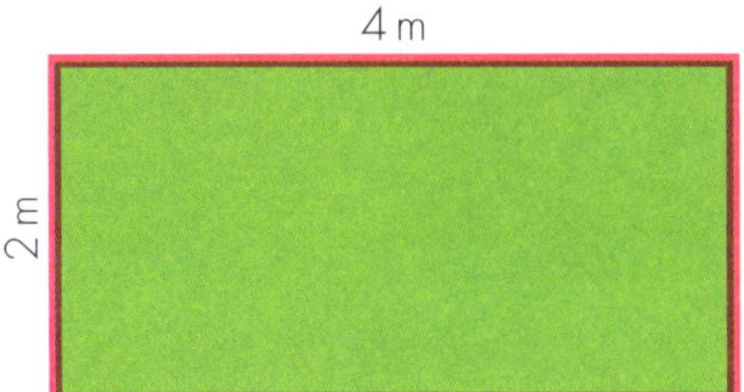

6 Look at the dimensions of the square and find its perimeter.

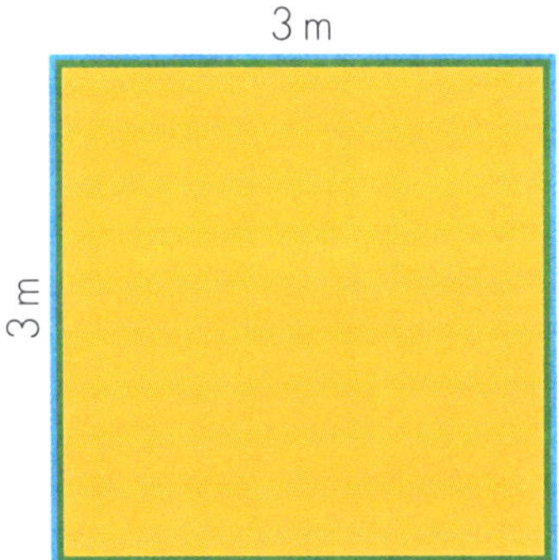

7 The perimeter of a square is 1 cm. Find the length of each side.

8 An ant walks around the edges of a rectangular tabletop. The table is 2 m long and 1 m wide. How far does the ant walk?

Perimeter and Length Problems

Use your addition and subtraction skills to solve these length and perimeter problems.

1. A washing machine and a dryer are each 26 in wide. What is their total width?

2. The distance between Akron and Barberton is 8 miles. If Peter cycled from Akron to Barberton and back again, how far did he cycle in total?

3. The perimeter of a rectangle is 30 cm. If the longer side is 8 cm, what is the length of the shorter side?

4. A rectangular parking lot is 70 yd long and 120 yd wide. What is the perimeter of the parking lot?

Time Filler:
Put together a small selection of cutlery such as spoons and serving forks. Estimate their lengths in inches and write them down. Now carefully measure each item and compare your estimates with the actual lengths.

5. A brick wall was 72 in high. A part of the wall was damaged in a storm. If the height of the wall is 48 in after the storm, how much height was lost?

6. Jack threw a ball a distance of 15 yd and Mary threw it a distance of 22 yd. How much farther did Mary throw the ball?

7. Write these lengths in inches.

2 ft

3 ft

1 ft 6 in

8. The perimeter of a square is 36 in. What is the length of each side?

Areas of Squares and Rectangles 1

Knowing your times tables will help you with area problems. Always be careful while writing the units.

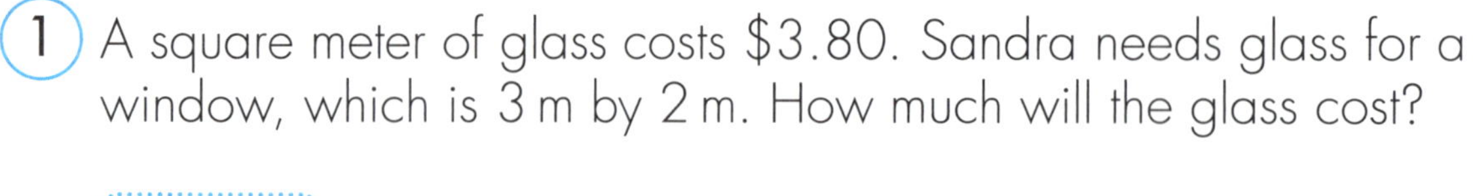

1. A square meter of glass costs \$3.80. Sandra needs glass for a window, which is 3 m by 2 m. How much will the glass cost?

2. The area of a square is 36 cm^2. What is the length of each side?

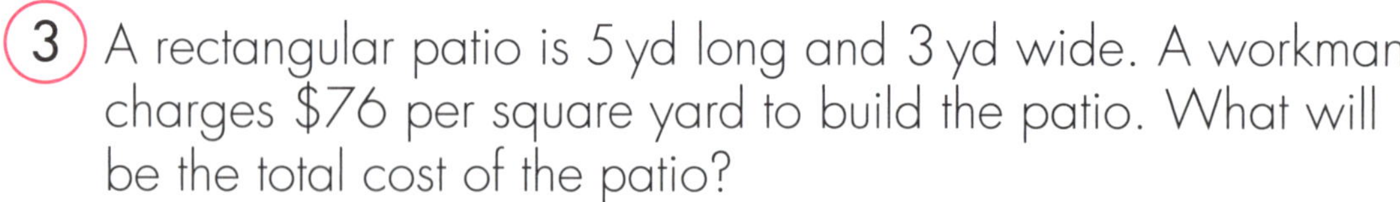

3. A rectangular patio is 5 yd long and 3 yd wide. A workman charges \$76 per square yard to build the patio. What will be the total cost of the patio?

4. A small can of paint can cover an area of 8 m^2. Katie needs to paint a wall that is 3 m high and 8 m wide. How many cans of paint will Katie need?

 cans

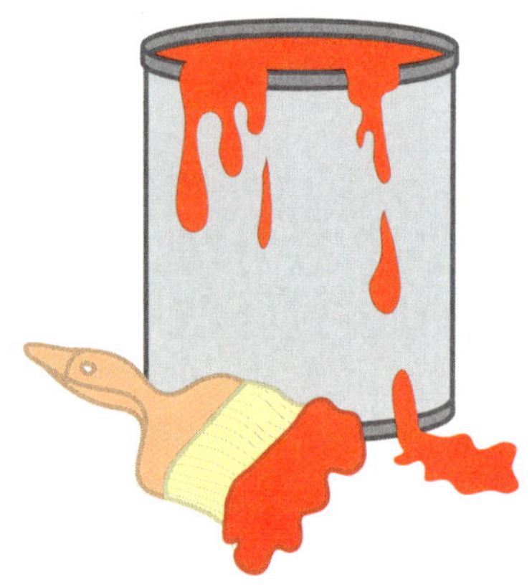

Time Filler:
Bring together some books of different sizes and arrange them in order according to the estimated area of the covers. Now measure the books in inches and find the areas of the covers.

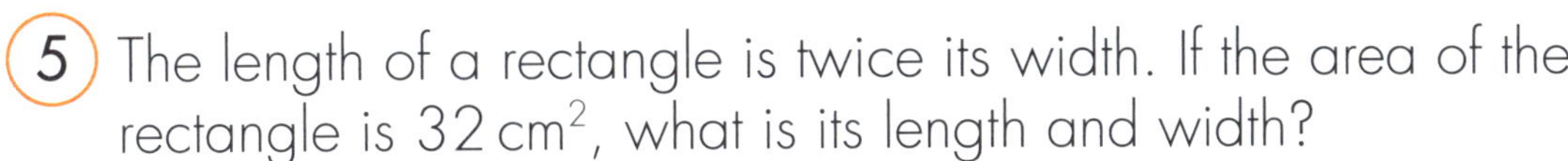

5. The length of a rectangle is twice its width. If the area of the rectangle is $32\,cm^2$, what is its length and width?

Length

Width

6. Look at the dimensions of the square and find its area.

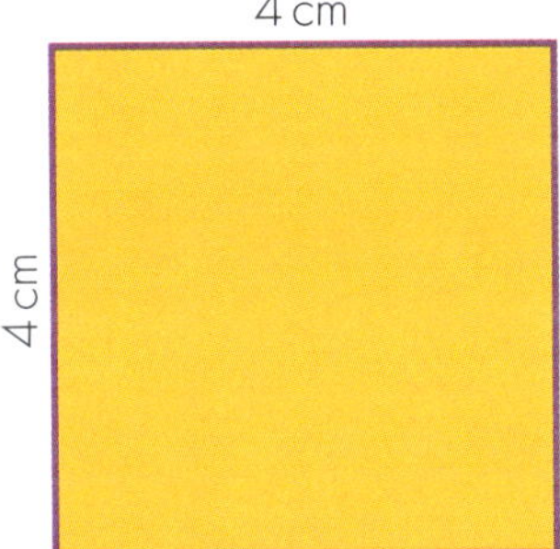

7. The sides of a square measure 3 in. The sides of another square are twice as long. What is the difference between the area of the two squares?

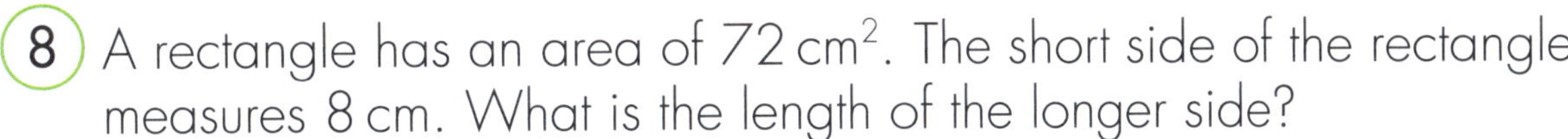

8. A rectangle has an area of $72\,cm^2$. The short side of the rectangle measures 8 cm. What is the length of the longer side?

Areas of Squares and Rectangles 2

Measure area using square units, such as square centimeter (cm^2), square meter (m^2), square inch (in^2), and square foot (ft^2).

1) Karen's parents want to lay a new carpet in her bedroom. The bedroom floor is 4 m long and 3 m wide.

What area of new carpet is required?

If the carpet costs $10 per square meter, how much will Karen's new bedroom carpet cost?

2) A builder draws the rectangular shape of a house he plans to build on graph paper. Look at his drawing below and the scale, and then calculate the area of the proposed house.

Scale
1 grid square = $1 m^2$

Area of house

3) A parking space in a garage is 4 m long and 2 m wide. What is the area of the parking space?

4) A square has an area of $144 cm^2$. What is the length of each side?

Time Filler:
Can you figure out the area of the floor in your bedroom? Measure the width and length to the nearest foot. If your floor area is not rectangular, you may want to ask an adult for help.

5) The area of a rectangle is $72\ ft^2$. If the width of the rectangle is 4 ft, then what is its length?

6) The width of a TV screen is 24 in and the height is 14 in. What is the area of the screen?

7) The area of a rectangle is $50\ in^2$. The length of the rectangle is two times its width. Calculate the length and the width of the rectangle.

Length

Width 

8) A table is placed in the center of a carpet that has an area of $9\ ft^2$. If the table has an area of $2\ ft^2$, what is the area of the carpet around the table?

Areas of Compound Shapes

When solving these problems, remember two half-squares can be counted as one square unit.

1) Peter's mom has to lay some new dirt in the garden. This diagram shows the shape she has to cover.

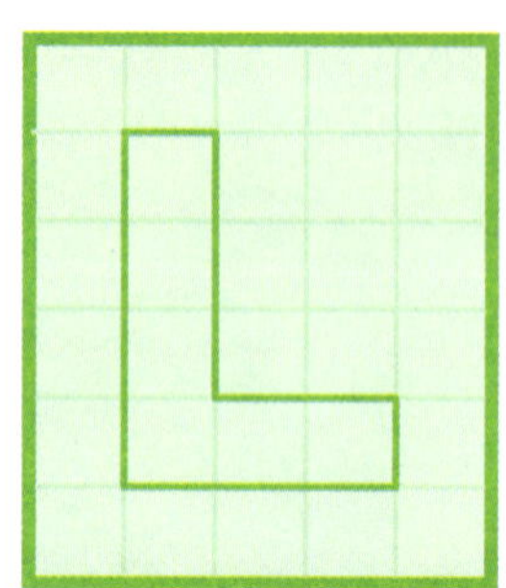

Scale

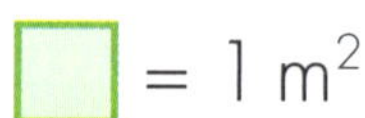 = 1 m^2

Count the squares and find the area that the new dirt will cover.

2) Dawn has to find the area of a shape she is using to make a model. This is the shape.

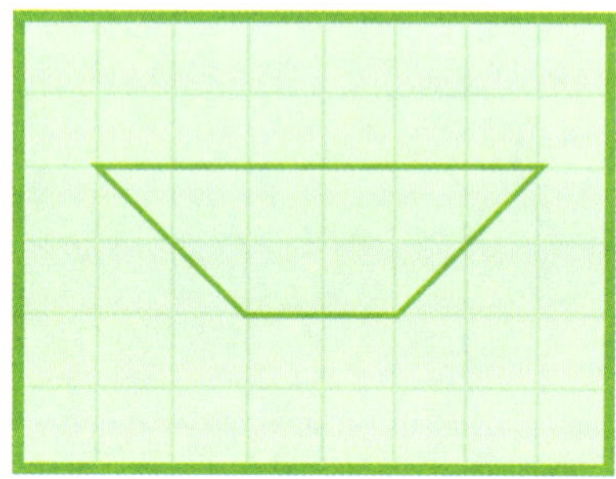

Scale

□ = 1 cm^2

Count the squares and find the area of Dawn's shape.

3) An area of road that has been damaged by heavy rain needs to be resurfaced.

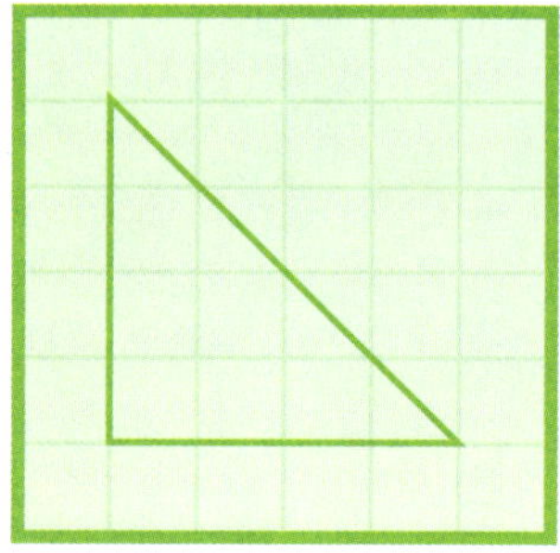

Scale

□ = 1 m^2

The diagram shows the area that has been damaged. Count the squares to find the area of damaged road.

Time Filler:
Look at any tiled areas in your home, such as in the kitchen or bathroom. See if there are any half or part squares, and decide how you would count them to calculate the total area.

4 What are the areas of these shapes?

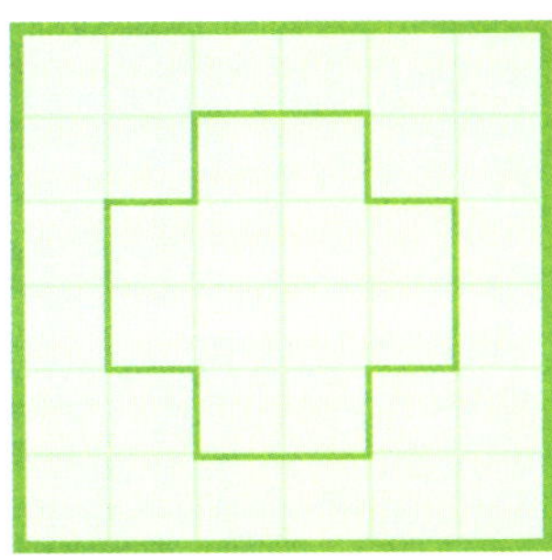

Scale
□ = 1 in^2

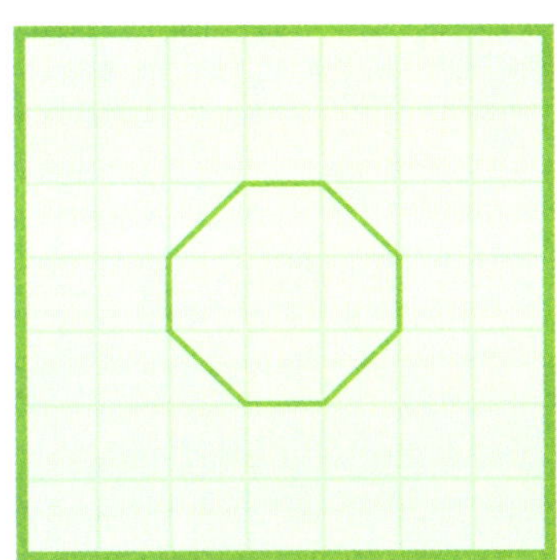

Scale
□ = 1 in^2

5 Jack's dad has decided to renovate his office. He makes the following drawing for it.

Scale
□ = 1 ft^2

What will be the area of his new office?

Weights and Measures 1

Can you remember how many ounces (oz) there are in a pound (lb)?

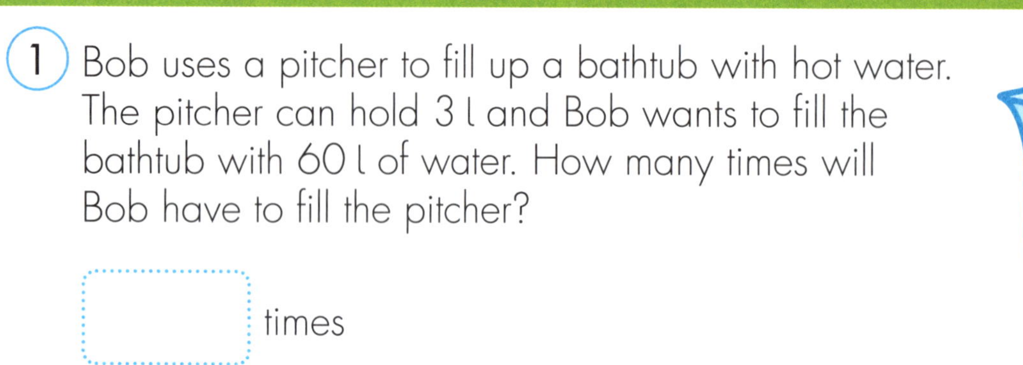

1) Bob uses a pitcher to fill up a bathtub with hot water. The pitcher can hold 3 l and Bob wants to fill the bathtub with 60 l of water. How many times will Bob have to fill the pitcher?

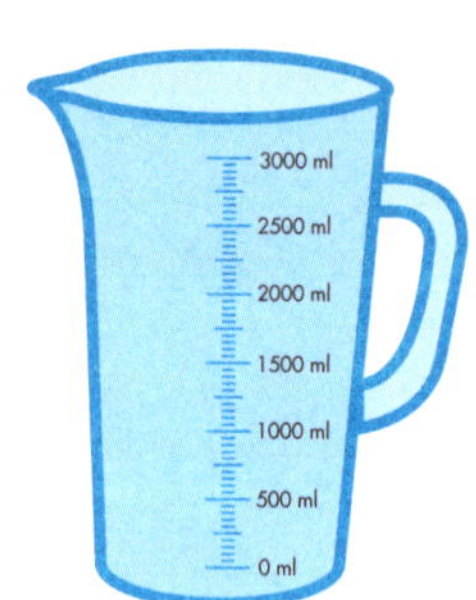

[ ] times

2) Jake has forgotten how many ounces are in a pound. He thinks 7 lb is the same as 700 oz, which is incorrect. Can you write the correct answer for him? How many ounces are in 7 lb?

[ ]

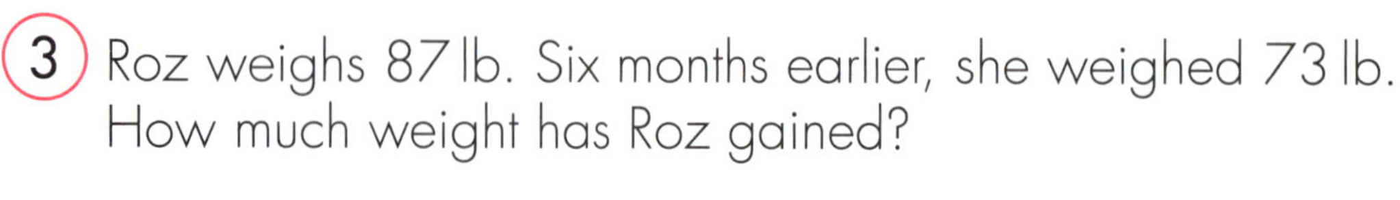

3) Roz weighs 87 lb. Six months earlier, she weighed 73 lb. How much weight has Roz gained?

4) Boris bought 3 lb of cherries. He figured out there were 25 cherries in 8 oz. How many cherries does Boris have altogether?

cherries

Time Filler:
Look at the recipes in some cookbooks. What units are the measurements in? See how many different units you can find.

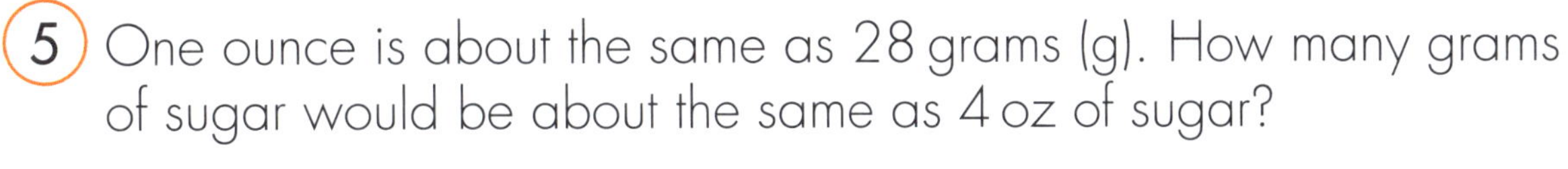

5 One ounce is about the same as 28 grams (g). How many grams of sugar would be about the same as 4 oz of sugar?

6 One box of cereal weighs 620 g and another weighs 480 g. What is the difference in their weights?

7 How many ounces are the same as 10 lb?

8 The maximum weight of a person allowed on a ride at an amusement park is 100 lb. Omar weighs 1,488 oz. Calculate his weight in pounds to find out if he will be allowed on the ride.

Will Omar be allowed on the ride? ....

Weights and Measures 2

Are you ready to tackle more problems about weights and measures? Let's go!

1. An empty soda bottle can hold 2 l of water. Sam is using the soda bottle to fill a bucket for a school project. He has filled the bottle and poured the water into the bucket five times. How many liters of water has Sam poured into the bucket?

2. An athlete is practicing for a long jump competition. Her first jump is 3 m long. Her second jump is 4 m long. By how much has she improved her jump?

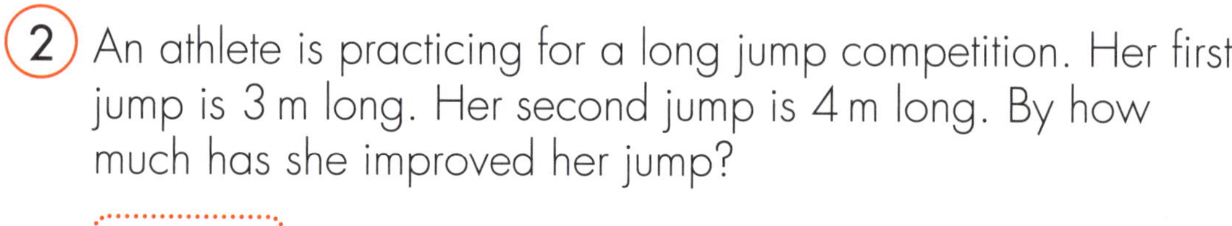

3. What is the difference in length between 62 cm and 104 cm?

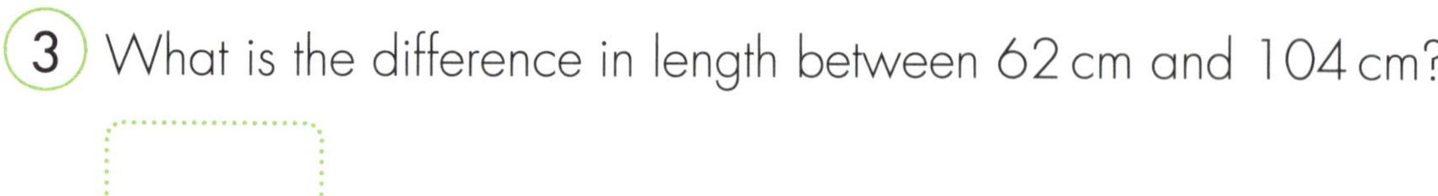

4. An Indian elephant weighs 6,000 lb. It picks up a log weighing 975 lb. What is the total weight of the elephant and the log?

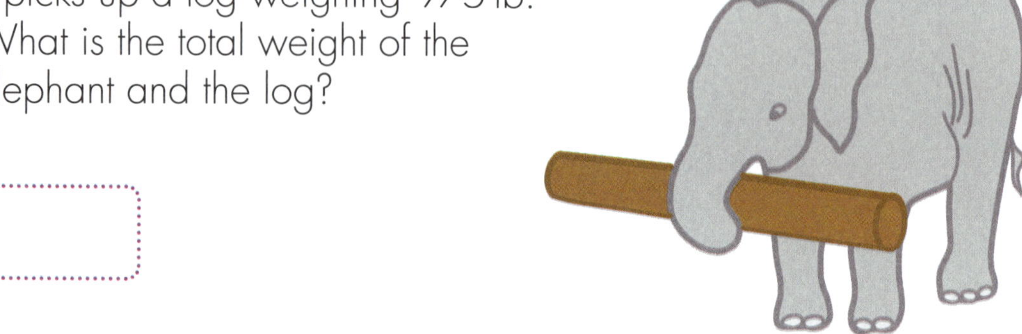

Time Filler:
In your kitchen, find fruits or vegetables of different sizes, such as a watermelon, a large potato, and an apple. Estimate each item's weight, and then weigh each item.

5) When Katie and her mother take their luggage to the airport, they are told the bag is too heavy. The bag weighs 60 lb but the allowance for luggage is only 52 lb. By how much have they exceeded the luggage allowance?

6) Jonah's dad runs at a speed of 11 mi per hour. How long will Jonah's dad take to run a distance of 22 mi?

7) Jennifer has six 1 l shampoo bottles. She gives two of them to Kim. How much shampoo does Jennifer have left? Write your answer in liters.

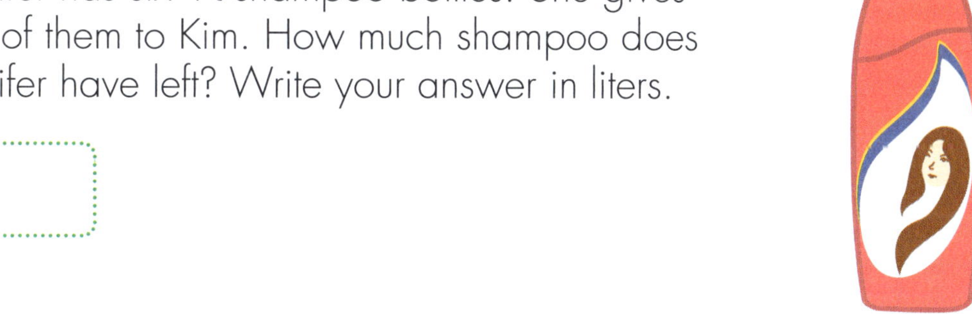

8) A teacher carried 12 books to his classroom. Each book weighed 8 oz. What was the total weight of the books? Write your answer in pounds.

Measurement Problems

Try these problems to see how well you understand measurements. Do not forget to check your answers.

1) Jamie leaves home at 9:50 AM and takes 25 minutes to walk to his school. At what time does Jamie reach school?

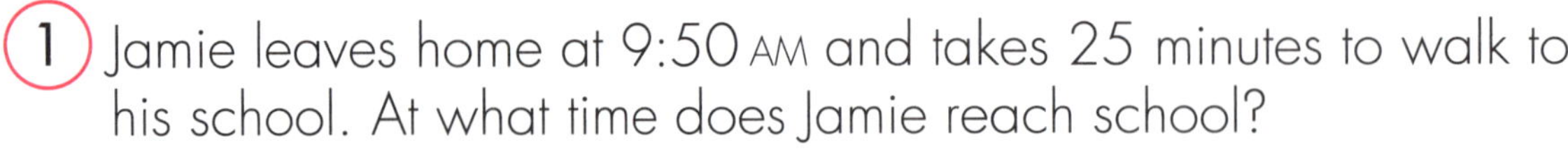

2) How many minutes are there between these times?

3) A jug holds 3 l of milk. If a mug holds half a liter of milk, how many mugs can be filled from the jug?

mugs

4) A bag of peanuts weighed 140 g. Mark ate all but 90 g of the peanuts. By how many grams has the weight of the bag decreased?

Time Filler:
Weigh yourself on a bathroom scale. Write your weight down to the nearest pound. Now see if you can figure out your weight in ounces. **Hint:** 1 pound (lb) is equal to 16 ounces (oz).

5. What is the area of this rectangle?

Scale

☐ = 1 cm^2

6. The perimeter of a square is 20 in. What is the length of each side of the box?

7. Brad drew a line that was 15 in long. His teacher had, however, asked him to draw a 7-inch-long line. By how much should Brad reduce the length of the line?

8. What is the difference between these two weights?

Money Problems 2

Get ready to practice some more money problems.

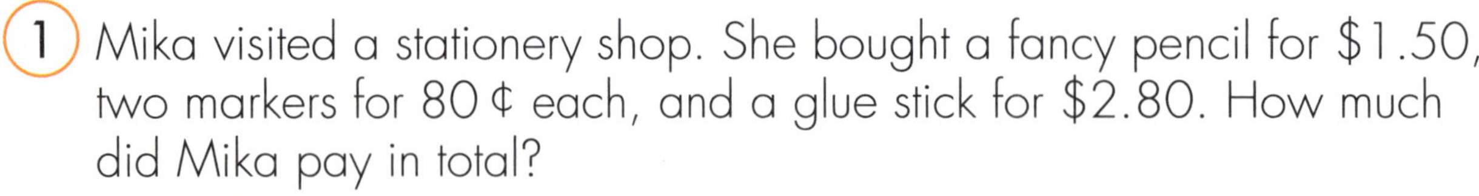

1) Mika visited a stationery shop. She bought a fancy pencil for $1.50, two markers for 80¢ each, and a glue stick for $2.80. How much did Mika pay in total?

2) Peter receives $5 allowance each week. Last week, he bought an ice cream for $1.40, lent $2 to his sister, and donated 50¢ to charity. He saved the rest of the money. How much did Peter save last week?

3) Isobel's class is raising money for charity. Twenty children donated $1 each, and nine children donated $1.50 each. How much money has the class raised so far?

4) Rob earns $13.50 an hour. At the end of a day, he had earned a total of $81. How many hours did Rob work that day?

Time Filler:
Do you know of other world currencies, like the euro (€), the yen (¥), and the pound (£)? Look them up in a book or on the Internet. Can you write your own equations using each currency?

5. A grocery bill amounts to $56.28. A quarter of the bill has been spent on fruit. How much money has not been spent on fruit?

6. Kevin bought 2 lb of tomatoes. The tomatoes cost $2.20 per lb. He gave the cashier a $10 bill. How much change should the cashier give him?

7. If one dollar will buy you five pieces of candy, how many pieces of candy can you buy with five dollars?

8. A taxi driver charges $2.30 per mi. If you travel a distance of 4 mi in his taxi, how much will your journey cost?

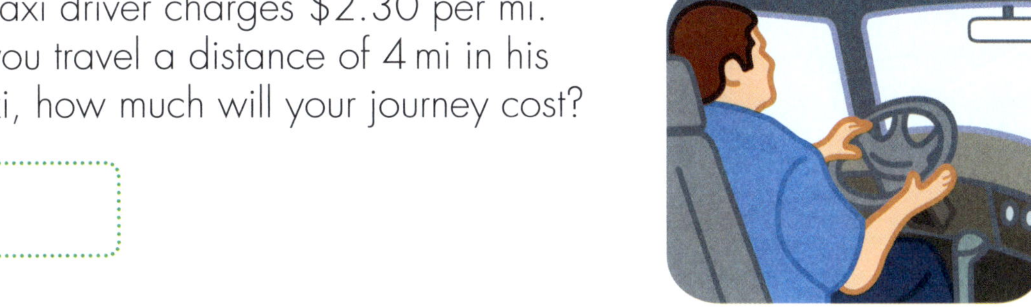

Understanding Graphs 1

Always look very carefully at the information shown on a graph before trying to solve the problems based on it.

Look at the graph below and answer the questions that follow.

1. What is the total time taken by all the children walking to school?

2. Which children take more time than Mary?

Time Filler:
Draw a graph to show some information about the children in your class. For example, the graph could show height, or number of brothers and sisters. Make sure the graph has a title and is labeled clearly.

3 Which two children take the same amount of time walking to school?

4 Which child takes the most time to reach school?

For how long does he or she travel?

5 How much longer than Ted does Sandra take?

6 If Ted cycles to school, he will take half the time to get there. How long will it take Ted take to cycle to school?

7 How much longer than Alice does Mary take?

8 One day, Sandra's grandmother gives her a ride to school. The ride takes only five minutes. How much time has Sandra managed to save that day?

Understanding Graphs 2

When you draw a bar graph, always make sure it has a title and is clearly labeled.

Ross wanted to find out what his friends ate for breakfast. He asked eight friends and wrote down what they had eaten that morning. The data below shows the information he collected.

Number of Friends	Type of Breakfast
4	Cereal
1	Egg
1	Fruit
2	Toast

1 Draw, label, and give a title to a bar graph to show Ross's information.

Time Filler:
Information, or data, is not always shown in bar graphs. Look in magazines, books, or on the Internet to see how many other kinds of graphs or charts you can find.

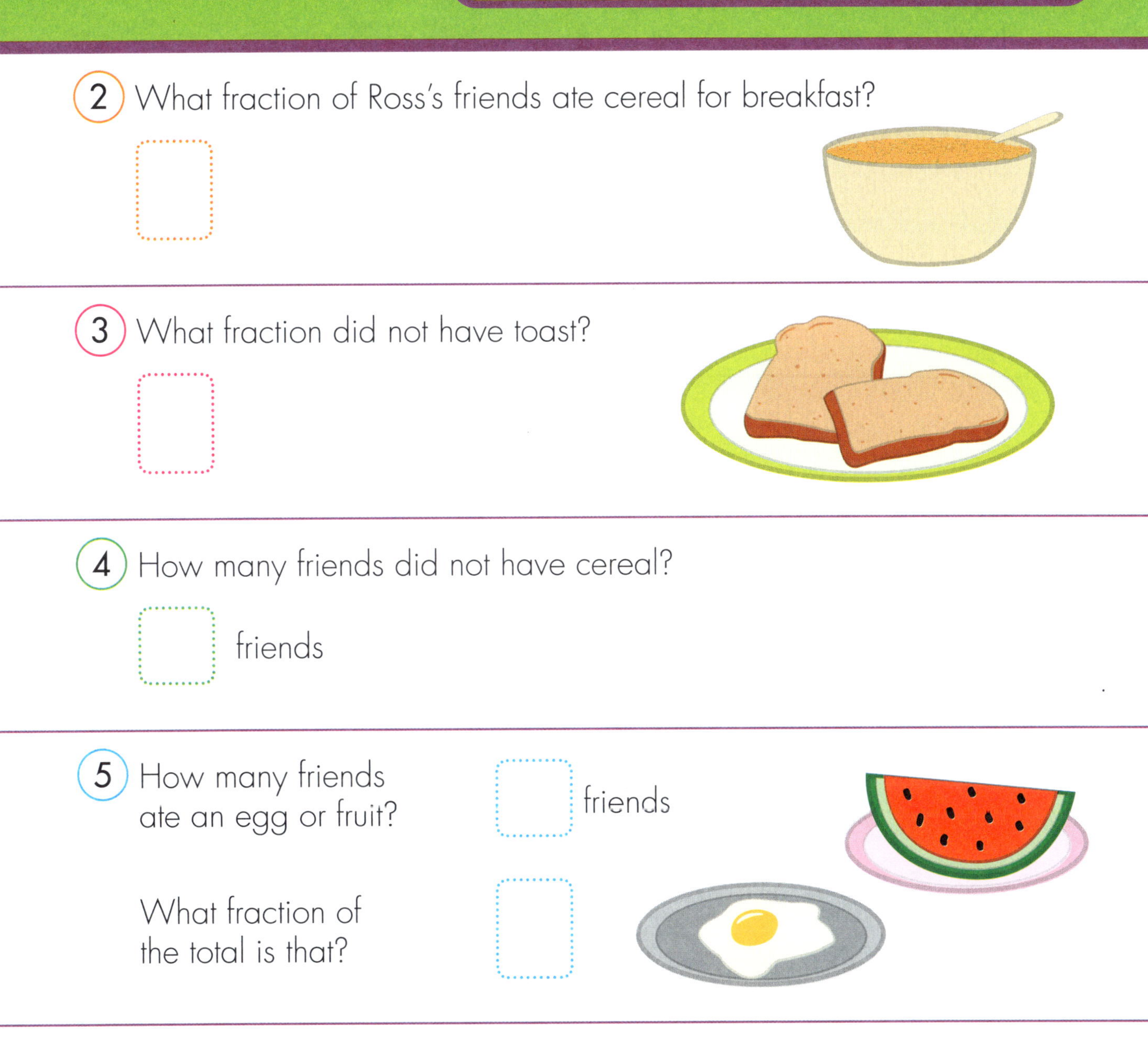

2 What fraction of Ross's friends ate cereal for breakfast?

3 What fraction did not have toast?

4 How many friends did not have cereal?

friends

5 How many friends ate an egg or fruit?

friends

What fraction of the total is that?

6 What fraction of the total ate cereal, an egg, or toast?

Addition and Subtraction 1

Test your addition and subtraction skills with these problems. Remember to check your answers.

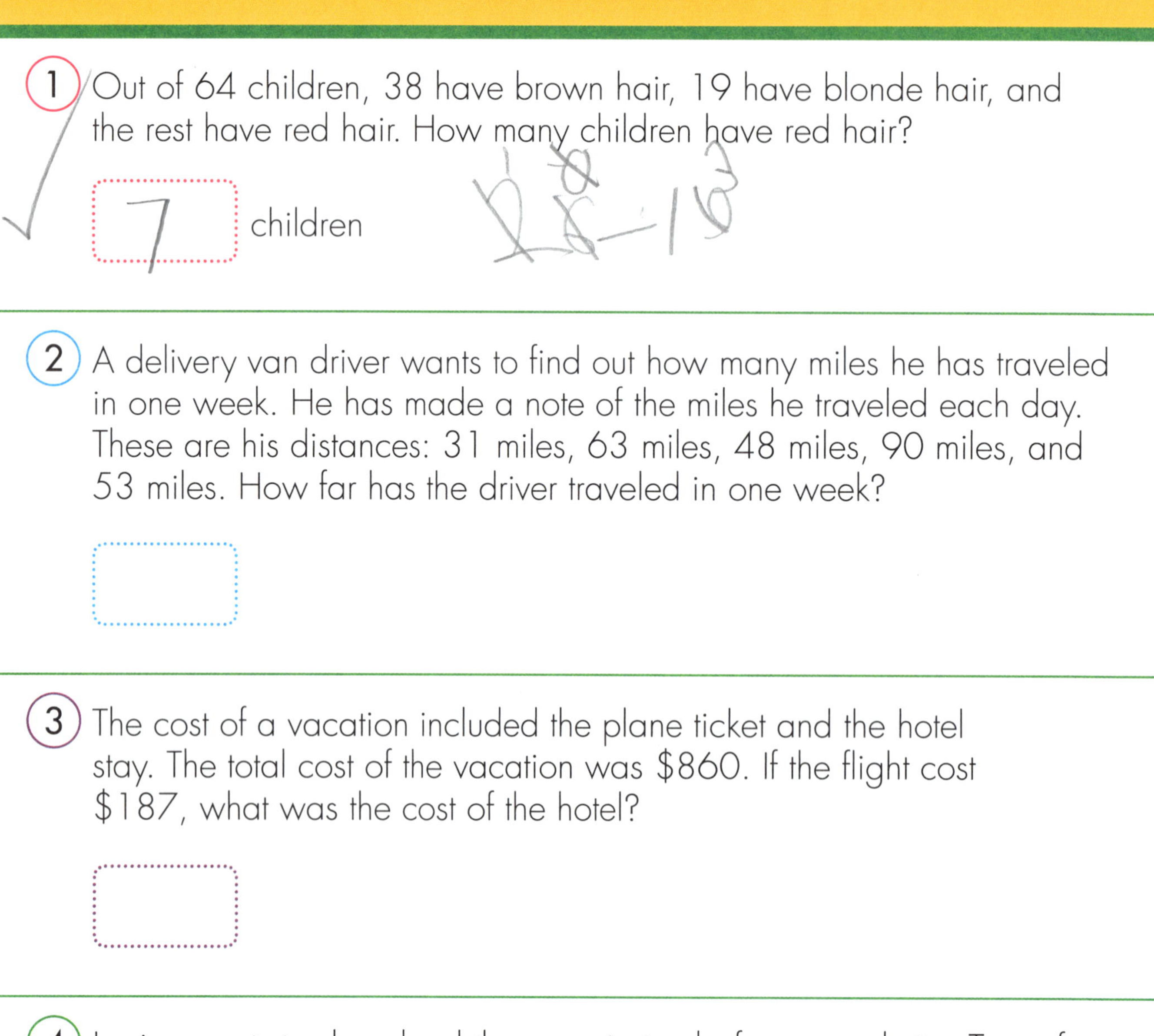

1. Out of 64 children, 38 have brown hair, 19 have blonde hair, and the rest have red hair. How many children have red hair?

   [ ] children

2. A delivery van driver wants to find out how many miles he has traveled in one week. He has made a note of the miles he traveled each day. These are his distances: 31 miles, 63 miles, 48 miles, 90 miles, and 53 miles. How far has the driver traveled in one week?

   [ ]

3. The cost of a vacation included the plane ticket and the hotel stay. The total cost of the vacation was \$860. If the flight cost \$187, what was the cost of the hotel?

   [ ]

4. Louise wants to download three music tracks from a website. Two of the tracks cost 79 ¢ each and the third one costs 99 ¢. How much will Louise have to pay for her music?

   [ ]

Time Filler:
Try this quick-fire problem: Add two and one and three and take two away. Now write your own quick-fire problems and ask your friends to answer them.

5 Katy subtracted a number from 150 and got the answer 89. What number did Katy subtract?

6 A bicycle race that is usually 27 km long is reduced by 9.5 km due to bad road conditions. How long is the race now?

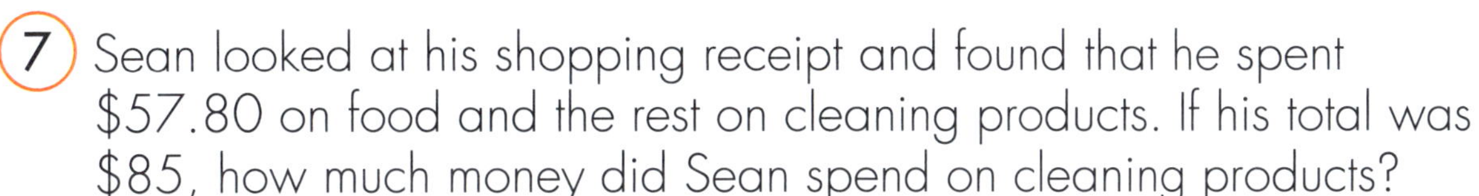

7 Sean looked at his shopping receipt and found that he spent $57.80 on food and the rest on cleaning products. If his total was $85, how much money did Sean spend on cleaning products?

8 A hotel room usually costs $110 for one night, but the manager reduces the price by $26 on Sunday nights. How much does the room cost on Sunday nights?

Addition and Subtraction 2

When you have finished solving an equation, double-check your answer.

1 Rashid, Sarah, and Mike are saving pennies for charity. In six months, Rashid has collected 90 pennies, Sarah has collected 50 pennies, and Mike has collected 60 pennies. How much money have they collected in total? Write your answer in dollars.

2 Farmer Frank has put his cattle into barns for winter. He moved 52 cows from one field, 45 cows from another field, and 63 cows from a third field. Each barn can hold 40 cows. How many barns did Frank use?

barns

3 A car had 30 gallons of gas in its tank. During a journey, 16 gallons of it was used up. How much gas is left in the tank?

4 Three consecutive numbers (numbers in a row) add up to 21. What are the numbers?

Time Filler:
A good way to check answers is to do the reverse operation; for example, if six plus seven is 13, then 13 minus six should be seven. Write five equations of your own, solve them, and then check each of them by doing the reverse operation.

5 Two suitcases are put on scales at an airport check-in counter. One suitcase weighs 42 lb. The total weight of both of them is 63 lb. How much does the other suitcase weigh?

6 One thousand pamphlets were printed for a local museum. Of these, 725 are in color, and the rest are black-and-white. How many black-and-white pamphlets were printed?

pamphlets

7 Jan thought of a number. She added 25 to it and then subtracted six. Her final number is 69. What number did Jan start with?

8 When Becky first played a computer game, she scored 478 points. On her second attempt, she scored 680 points. How many more points did Becky score on her second attempt?

points

Addition and Subtraction 3

Some of these problems are tricky.
Make sure to read each one carefully!

1. When David added three numbers together, he arrived at a total of 68. The first of the numbers is 12. The second number is double the first number. What is the third number?

2. Emmie has a collection of 600 CDs. She has decided to give some away. If Emmie gives away 48 CDs, how many will she have left?

 CDs

3. Sean wants to give some money to a basketball fund. He finds 78 ¢ in his wallet and 54 ¢ in his bedroom drawer. He decides to give $1 of the money he found to the fund. How much money will Sean keep for himself?

4. The total of three numbers is 1,000. If 80 and 250 are two of the numbers, what is the third number?

Time Filler:
Write down some numbers in numerical order, add them up, and write the answer. Now add them up again, but this time in the reverse order. Is the answer the same?

5. In a tin of 90 cookies, 34 are broken. How many cookies are not broken?

[ ] cookies

6. Petra's mom has 86 e-mails in her inbox, but 49 of them are unwanted spam. How many e-mails are not unwanted spam?

[ ] e-mails

7. Gale added two numbers together and got 240. If one of the numbers is 165, what is the other number?

8. Seventy pages of a notebook have been used up. If the notebook has 130 pages, how many blank pages are left?

[ ] pages

Multiplication and Division 1

Make sure you read the problems carefully before attempting them. A quick recall of times tables will be very helpful.

1. A standard running track is 400 m long. If an athlete goes around the track four times, how far will she have run? Write your answer in kilometers. **Hint:** 1 km = 1,000 m

2. Ben organized a party and invited nine friends as guests. Each guest ate four small sandwiches. How many sandwiches did the guests eat altogether?

 sandwiches

3. Marcel has to divide his postcard collection equally among his five children. If Marcel has a collection of 150 postcards, how many will each child receive?

postcards

4. Sixty library books need to be put in piles of 12. How many piles of books will there be?

piles

Time Filler:
Write down a few multiplication problems, then write the inverse problems for each. For example, first write 6 x 3 = 18, then write its inverse problems: 18 ÷ 6 = 3 and 18 ÷ 3 = 6.

5 A number multiplied by seven is 63. What is the number?

6 Each text message Erica sends costs her 6 ¢. If Erica sends 40 messages in one month, how much will they cost her in total? Write your answer in dollars and cents.

7 If three times 15 is 45, what will six times 15 be?

8 Marie planted tulips in her garden. She planted three rows with 12 tulips in each row. How many tulips did Marie plant in all?

tulips

Multiplication and Division 2

Use these problems to help brush up your multiplication and division skills.

1 In a video game, a player is awarded 15 points every time the frog catches a fly, and 20 points when the frog catches a wasp. How many points will a player earn if the frog catches six flies and nine wasps?

[ ] points

2 Charlie has saved 50 ¢ every day for 21 days. How much money has Charlie saved in total? Write your answer in dollars and cents.

[ ]

3 A teacher graded 64 test booklets every evening for six days. How many booklets did the teacher grade in total?

[ ] booklets

4 Pat went to the gym 132 times in a year. If she went an equal number of times each month, how many gym visits did she make each month?

[ ] times

Time Filler:
Time to sharpen your mental arithmetic! Think of any number between 12 and 20 and write it down. Now figure out several multiples of this number in your head. Do the same with a few other numbers.

5 A parcel delivery company has 520 parcels to be delivered by four drivers. How many parcels will each driver need to deliver?

☐ parcels

6 Victor thinks of a number that is seven times smaller than 56. Which number is he thinking of?

☐

7 Debbie multiplied a number by itself and got 81 as the product. Which number did Debbie start with?

☐

8 A birthday cake is covered with chocolate candies and cut into eight pieces. Each piece has 6 candies except one piece, which has 7. How many chocolate candies were put on the cake?

☐ candies

Multiplication and Division 3

Knowing your times tables is the key to solving these problems quickly.

1. A teacher started a math lesson by writing 10 equations on the board and asking the students to solve them. That evening, the teacher checked the students' answers. If the class has 30 children, how many answers did the teacher have to check?

   answers

2. Mrs. Harris has collected 68 fridge magnets over the years. She decided to buy a smaller fridge, so she distributed the magnets equally between Molly, Isaac, Louis, and Isabel. How many fridge magnets did each child receive?

   magnets

3. A driver collects 10 bonus points every time he spends $1 on gas. If the driver spent $55 on gas, how many bonus points did he collect?

   points

4. Markers come in packets of 20. How many markers will there be in a dozen packets?

   markers

Time Filler:
Empty your piggy bank or money box. Put all the different coins—pennies, nickels, dimes, etc.—into separate piles and count each pile. Then add them together to find out the grand total.

5) Kim divided a number by 12 and arrived at an answer of 15. What number did Kim start with?

6) The captain of a ship loaded 600 containers in 12 rows. How many containers are there in each row?

containers

7) Ninety pieces of candy are divided among a number of children. If each child receives 15 pieces, how many children are there?

children

8) Eighty-four bananas are shared equally among 12 people. How many bananas does each person get?

bananas

Money Problems 3

With practice, you will find these money problems easy to solve.

1. Convert these amounts of money from cents to dollars.

1,000 ¢		700 ¢	
250 ¢		100 ¢	

2. \$4 was shared equally among 5 children. How much money did each child receive?

3. William and Kate added their money together and then shared it equally among themselves and their son, George. If William had \$3.50 and Kate had \$5.50, how much money did George receive after the money was shared?

4. Claire, Bruno, Mark, and Ella went for lunch together. They shared the bill of \$20.60 equally among themselves. How much money did each of them pay?

Time Filler:
Use the Internet to find the conversion rate between the dollar ($) and the euro (€). If you had one dollar in the United States, how many euros would that equal?

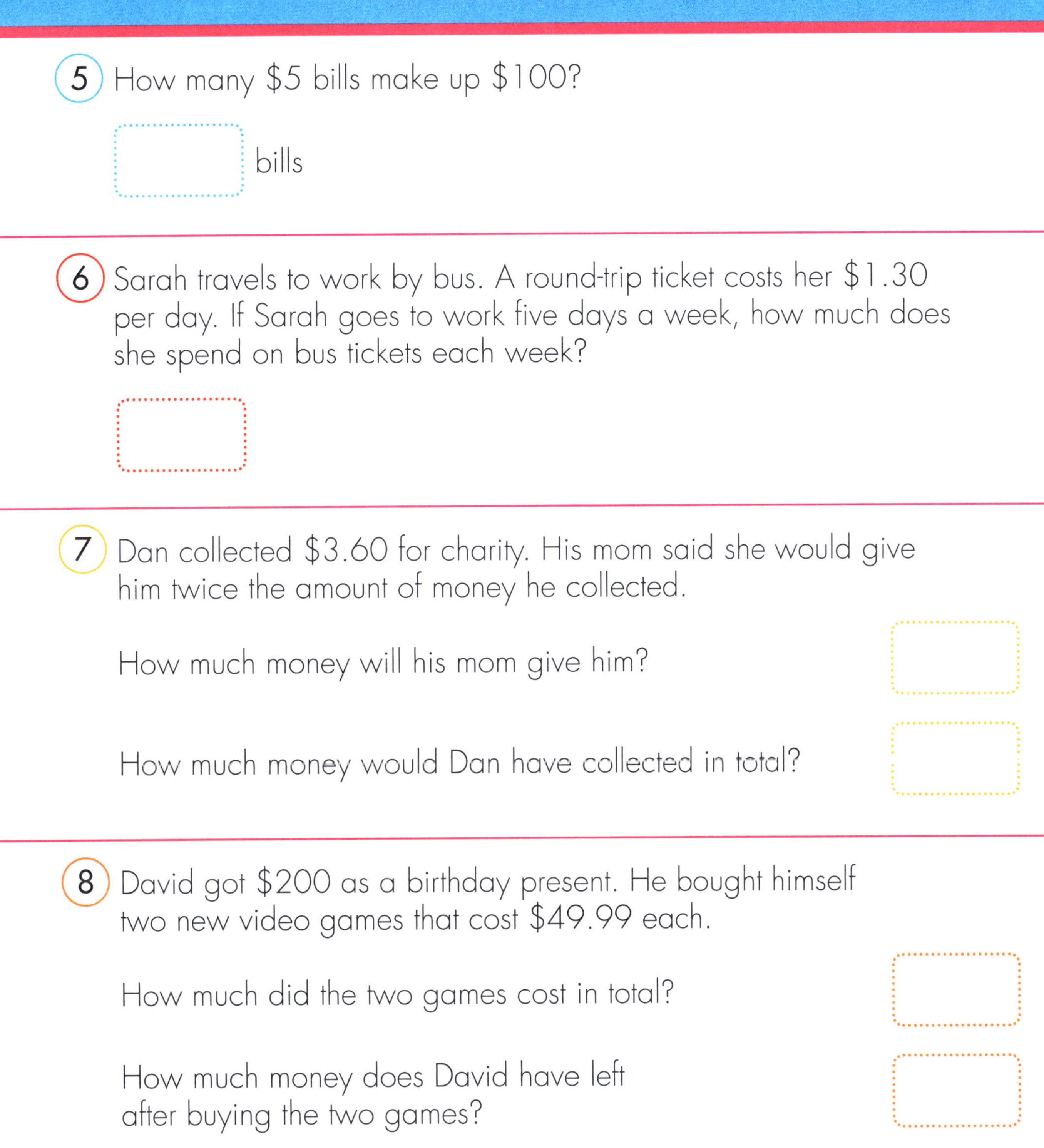

5 How many $5 bills make up $100?

bills

6 Sarah travels to work by bus. A round-trip ticket costs her $1.30 per day. If Sarah goes to work five days a week, how much does she spend on bus tickets each week?

7 Dan collected $3.60 for charity. His mom said she would give him twice the amount of money he collected.

How much money will his mom give him?

How much money would Dan have collected in total?

8 David got $200 as a birthday present. He bought himself two new video games that cost $49.99 each.

How much did the two games cost in total?

How much money does David have left after buying the two games?

Times Tables Problems 1

Practice with times tables will help you do calculations in your mind.

1. If four eights are 32, what will eight eights be?

2. How many days are equal to eight weeks?

   days

3. Kara doubled the number four and then doubled it again. At what result did she arrive?

4. Dan arranged cupcakes on a tray in three rows of five. How many cupcakes are there on the tray?

Time Filler:
How old are you in years? Say aloud the times table for that number. For example, if you are seven years old, say your seven times table. Now say aloud the times table for the age you will be on your next birthday.

5 Callum halved a number and the result was 16. What was the original number?

6 When five is multiplied by a number, the answer is 60. What is the number?

7 If twelve times twelve is 144, what will six times twelve be?

8 What is the product of three times three times three?

9 If 12 fours are 48, what will six fours be?

Times Tables Problems 2

If you have your times tables memorized, you will solve these problems quickly!

1. Billy is 7 years old, and Mandy is 12 years old.
How many months old are they?

Billy is [ ] months old. Mandy is [ ] months old.

2. A boy earns $15 per day shoveling snow in the winter.

If he works five days a week, how much will he earn? [ ]

If he works seven days a week and gets an extra $2 for each day of weekend work, how much will he earn? [ ]

3. It costs Jill $12 each time she has a piano lesson.
If Jill has nine lessons, how much will they cost her in total?

[ ]

In the summer, the cost of each piano lesson drops. If Jill has eight summer lessons and they cost her a total of $72, how much does each lesson cost?

[ ]

Time Filler:
Write down these numbers: 24, 60, 72, 90. Now write down all of their multiplication combinations. For example, 72 can be an answer to 6 x 12 as well as 2 x 36.

4. For a party, five children collect eight pairs of sunglasses each. How many pairs of sunglasses do they have altogether?

   ☐ pairs of sunglasses

5. How many days are there in nine weeks?

   ☐ days

6. Seven children have collected eight party hats each. What is the total number of hats they have for the party?

   ☐ hats

7. How many months are there in five years?

   ☐ months

8. A teacher has drawn six octagons on the board. How many sides has he drawn in total?

   ☐ sides

Times Tables Problems 3

Remember, knowing your times tables will help with multiplication and division!

1. Daniel bought eight boxes of chocolates to take on a vacation. Each box contains 12 chocolates. How many chocolates does Daniel have in total?

   ☐ chocolates

2. William multiplied two by three. He multiplied the answer by four and then doubled it. Finally, he divided that answer by four. Which number did William finish with?

   ☐

3. Adam knows only two single-digit numbers can be multiplied to make 63, but he cannot remember the numbers. What are the two numbers Adam is trying to remember?

   ☐ and ☐

4. Anna Elizabeth doubled a number. She then doubled the result and got 32. Which number did Anna Elizabeth start with?

   ☐

Time Filler:
Some numbers can only be a multiple of one and themselves. For example, 1 x 7 = 7, but no other numbers can be multiplied to reach 7. Numbers like these are called *prime numbers*. Can you find five other examples of a prime number?

5 Which number multiplied by four gives the same answer as six times six?

6 The product of which two single-digit numbers gives 35?

and

7 Multiply the number of days in a week by the number of months in a year.

8 A packet contains eight cookies. Jessica wants 48 cookies to share with her friends. How many packets will she need?

Harder Problems 1

Are you ready for these brainteasers? You've had lots of practice, so let's go!

1. A number is multiplied by its double. The answer is 72. What is the number?

2. A farmer has 180 ewes on his farm. In spring, each of them gives birth to two lambs. How many ewes and lambs will there now be on the farm?

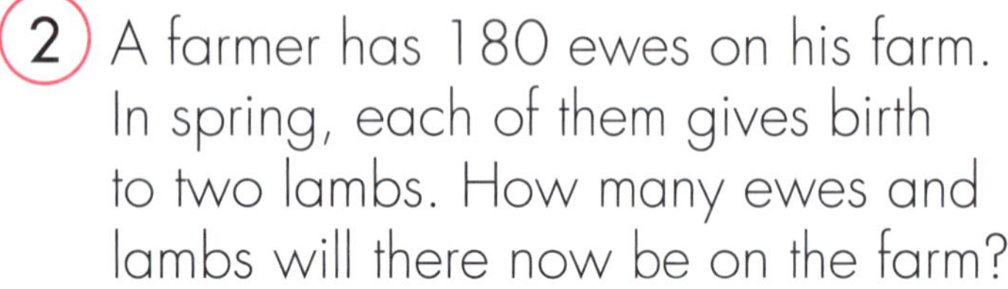

ewes and lambs

3. The sum of two numbers is 15. The product of these numbers is 54. What are the two numbers?

and

4. Martin and Marie go jogging. Martin jogs twice as far as Marie. If they cover a combined distance of 12 mi, how far does each of them jog?

Martin

Marie

Time Filler:
Write some number problems of your own and ask your family members to solve them. Be sure to make them extra tricky! You may choose to give a prize to the fastest solver.

5) James spends 84¢ on candy. He pays for it with a $1 bill and receives three different coins as change. What are the values of the coins?

6) A number is doubled first and then doubled again. All three numbers are then added together and the total is 49. What is the original number?

7) Cathy and Sean go fishing and catch 12 fish altogether. If Cathy catches three times as many fish as Sean, how many fish does each child catch?

Cathy catches ☐ fish

Sean catches ☐ fish

8) The total of two numbers is 21 and the difference between them is three. What are the two numbers?

☐ and ☐

Harder Problems 2

Read each problem very carefully, then decide what needs to be done.

1. Find the total of these numbers. Can you figure out a quick way of adding them?

   0, 1, 2, 3, 4, 5, 6, 7, 8, 9, 10

2. Allie multiplied a number by itself and then halved it. The answer was 18. Which number did Allie begin with?

3. Dr. Foster's appointments with her patients last eight minutes. After each appointment, she takes a two-minute break. How many appointments can Dr. Foster have in one hour?

patients

4. Corey went to the movie theater to see the latest animated film, which is 1 hour 55 minutes long. The film ended at 1:30 PM. What time did it begin?

Time Filler:
Look at this problem: 12 + 3 – 4 + 5 + 67 + 8 + 9 = 100. What do you notice? Look on the Internet for more fun math facts. Can you find out the name for the number that is one followed by one hundred zeroes?

5) Peter spends twice as much on clothes as Marilyn does. If Marilyn spends $24, how much do they spend in total?

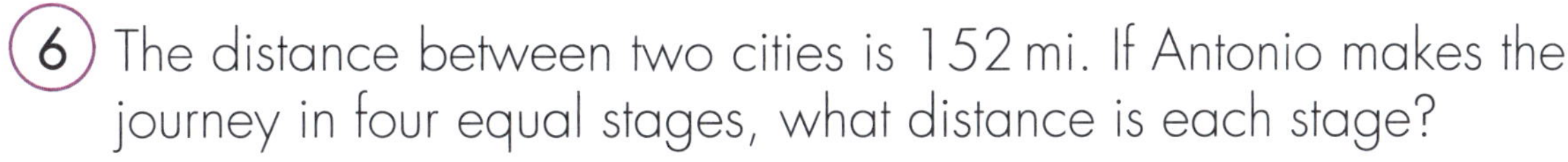

6) The distance between two cities is 152 mi. If Antonio makes the journey in four equal stages, what distance is each stage?

7) Marianne goes to bed at 11:30 PM and sleeps for 10 hours. What time does Marianne wake up?

8) Zen makes his favorite drink by mixing orange juice and water. If he uses 225 ml of orange juice and twice that amount of water, how much drink will he have?

Answers:

04–05 Seconds, Minutes, and Hours

06–07 Days, Weeks, and Months

4

1 How many seconds are there in one hour?

3,600 seconds

2 How many minutes are there in one day?

1,440 minutes

3 Amir takes 20 minutes to walk to school. His sister Cala takes 25 minutes to walk the same distance. When their father takes them to school by car, the journey takes only six minutes. How many minutes does each child gain by being driven to school?

Amir gains 14 minutes Cala gains 19 minutes

4 Sam takes 1 hour 50 minutes to walk home. It is five times quicker for him if he takes a bus home. How long does it take Sam to get home by bus?

22 minutes

5 Add together the number of minutes in one hour, three-quarters of an hour, half an hour, and a quarter of an hour.

150 minutes

6 Terry likes his eggs to be boiled for 270 seconds. How long is that in minutes and seconds?

4 minutes 30 seconds

7 Henry and Francine used a timer to record the time it took them to beat a computer game. Henry beat the game in 2 minutes 38 seconds, and Francine beat the game in 1 minute 42 seconds. How much quicker is Francine than Henry?

56 seconds

8 It took Dani 3 hours 45 minutes to complete the first ten levels of a new video game. Alex, however, completed them in only 55 minutes. How much quicker was Alex than Dani?

2 hours 50 minutes

5

Your child should learn simple multiples of 60 and 24, such as 5 x 60 and 8 x 24, to be able to quickly convert between minutes and seconds, hours and minutes, and days and hours.

6

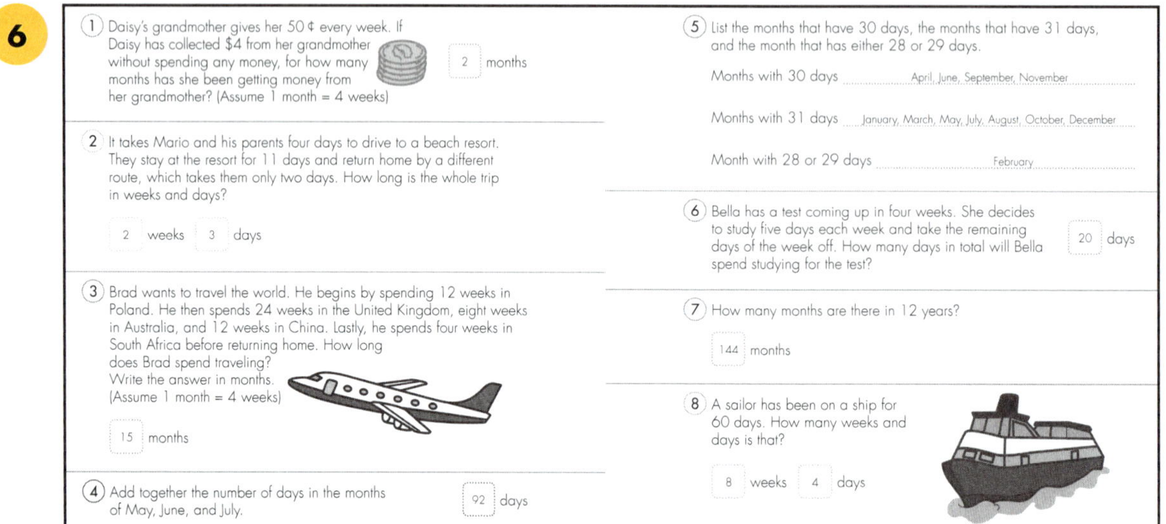

1 Daisy's grandmother gives her 50¢ every week. If Daisy has collected $4 from her grandmother without spending any money, for how many months has she been getting money from her grandmother? (Assume 1 month = 4 weeks)

2 months

2 It takes Mario and his parents four days to drive to a beach resort. They stay at the resort for 11 days and return home by a different route, which takes them only two days. How long is the whole trip in weeks and days?

2 weeks 3 days

3 Brad wants to travel the world. He begins by spending 12 weeks in Poland. He then spends 24 weeks in the United Kingdom, eight weeks in Australia, and 12 weeks in China. Lastly, he spends four weeks in South Africa before returning home. How long does Brad spend traveling? Write the answer in months. (Assume 1 month = 4 weeks)

15 months

4 Add together the number of days in the months of May, June, and July.

92 days

5 List the months that have 30 days, the months that have 31 days, and the month that has either 28 or 29 days.

Months with 30 days April, June, September, November

Months with 31 days January, March, May, July, August, October, December

Month with 28 or 29 days February

6 Bella has a test coming up in four weeks. She decides to study five days each week and take the remaining days of the week off. How many days in total will Bella spend studying for the test?

20 days

7 How many months are there in 12 years?

144 months

8 A sailor has been on a ship for 60 days. How many weeks and days is that?

8 weeks 4 days

7

Your child should readily know the number of days in each month of the year. He or she should also be able to quickly change a certain number of days into weeks. For example, 63 days can be converted into 9 weeks.

Answers:

08–09 Years, Decades, and Centuries
10–11 Time Problems 1

8

1 A crack in a wall lengthens by 1 in each year. If the crack is 3 in long now, how long will it be after…

1 year? 4 in 1 decade? 13 in

2 Jacob was born in 2004.

How old will Jacob be in the year 2017? 13 years

Will Jacob be 50 in the 2040s, 2050s, or 2060s? 2050s

3 Here is a list of some famous events in American history. Look at the years in which they happened. Write the year a century before and a century after each event.

Event	Year	Century Before	Century After
Louisiana Purchase	1803	1703	1903
Beginning of the Civil War	1861	1761	1961
Apollo 11 moon landing	1969	1869	2069

9

4 What is the year a decade before each of these years?

2008	1990	2003
1998	1980	1993

5 What is the year a decade after each of these years?

1972	1995	2015
1982	2005	2025

6 What is the year a century before each of these years?

1918	1999	2015
1818	1899	1915

7 What is the year a century after each of these years?

980	1999	1968
1080	2099	2068

8 What name do we give to a period of 1,000 years? a millennium

Your child should have the idea of years, decades, and centuries at his or her fingertips. It may also be useful if he or she knows how to write numbers and years in Roman numerals.

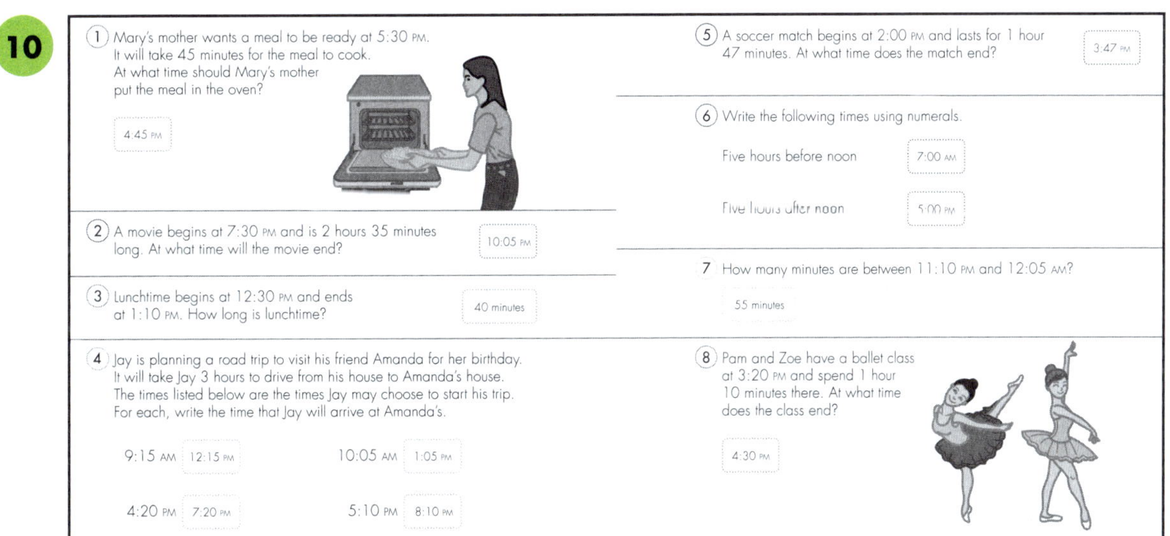

10

1 Mary's mother wants a meal to be ready at 5:30 PM. It will take 45 minutes for the meal to cook. At what time should Mary's mother put the meal in the oven?

4:45 PM

2 A movie begins at 7:30 PM and is 2 hours 35 minutes long. At what time will the movie end? 10:05 PM

3 Lunchtime begins at 12:30 PM and ends at 1:10 PM. How long is lunchtime? 40 minutes

4 Jay is planning a road trip to visit his friend Amanda for her birthday. It will take Jay 3 hours to drive from his house to Amanda's house. The times listed below are the times Jay may choose to start his trip. For each, write the time that Jay will arrive at Amanda's.

9:15 AM 12:15 PM 10:05 AM 1:05 PM

4:20 PM 7:20 PM 5:10 PM 8:10 PM

11

5 A soccer match begins at 2:00 PM and lasts for 1 hour 47 minutes. At what time does the match end? 3:47 PM

6 Write the following times using numerals.

Five hours before noon 7:00 AM

Five hours after noon 5:00 PM

7 How many minutes are between 11:10 PM and 12:05 AM?

55 minutes

8 Pam and Zoe have a ballet class at 3:20 PM and spend 1 hour 10 minutes there. At what time does the class end?

4:30 PM

It may interest your child that some people use a different time system, called the 24-hour clock (also known as military time), to show time. In this system, for example, 9:30 AM is written as 09:30, 4:00 PM as 16:00, and midnight as either 00:00 or 24:00.

Answers:

12–13 Time Problems 2

14–15 Money Problems 1, see p.80

16–17 Length Problems 1

12

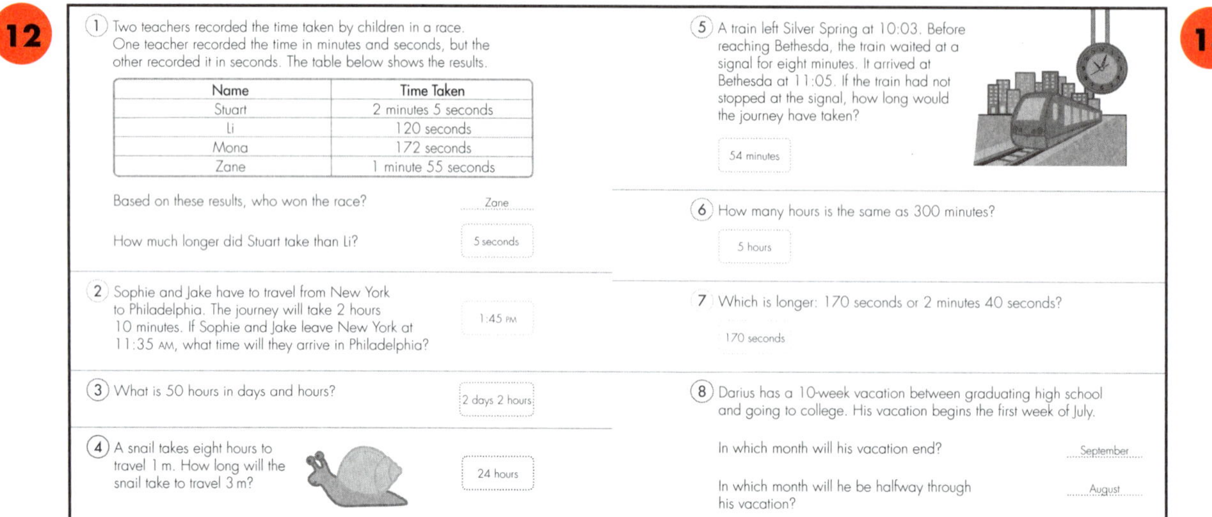

(1) Two teachers recorded the time taken by children in a race. One teacher recorded the time in minutes and seconds, but the other recorded it in seconds. The table below shows the results.

Name	Time Taken
Stuart	2 minutes 5 seconds
Li	120 seconds
Mona	172 seconds
Zane	1 minute 55 seconds

Based on these results, who won the race? Zane

How much longer did Stuart take than Li? 5 seconds

(2) Sophie and Jake have to travel from New York to Philadelphia. The journey will take 2 hours 10 minutes. If Sophie and Jake leave New York at 11:35 AM, what time will they arrive in Philadelphia? 1:45 PM

(3) What is 50 hours in days and hours? 2 days 2 hours

(4) A snail takes eight hours to travel 1 m. How long will the snail take to travel 3 m? 24 hours

(5) A train left Silver Spring at 10:03. Before reaching Bethesda, the train waited at a signal for eight minutes. It arrived at Bethesda at 11:05. If the train had not stopped at the signal, how long would the journey have taken? 54 minutes

(6) How many hours is the same as 300 minutes? 5 hours

(7) Which is longer: 170 seconds or 2 minutes 40 seconds? 170 seconds

(8) Darius has a 10-week vacation between graduating high school and going to college. His vacation begins the first week of July.

In which month will his vacation end? September

In which month will he be halfway through his vacation? August

13

It is important to encourage your child to try to visualize the situations represented in each math problem. If your child can clearly imagine the scenario, he or she is more likely to be able to solve the problem.

16

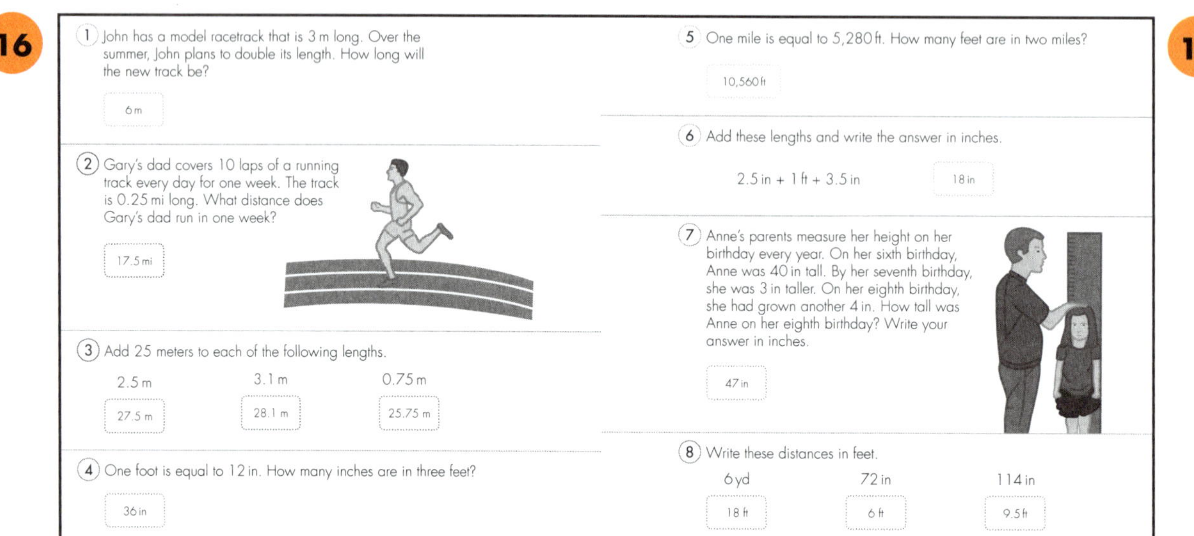

(1) John has a model racetrack that is 3 m long. Over the summer, John plans to double its length. How long will the new track be? 6 m

(2) Gary's dad covers 10 laps of a running track every day for one week. The track is 0.25 mi long. What distance does Gary's dad run in one week? 17.5 mi

(3) Add 25 meters to each of the following lengths.

2.5 m — 27.5 m
3.1 m — 28.1 m
0.75 m — 25.75 m

(4) One foot is equal to 12 in. How many inches are in three feet? 36 in

(5) One mile is equal to 5,280 ft. How many feet are in two miles? 10,560 ft

(6) Add these lengths and write the answer in inches.

2.5 in + 1 ft + 3.5 in — 18 in

(7) Anne's parents measure her height on her birthday every year. On her sixth birthday, Anne was 40 in tall. By her seventh birthday, she was 3 in taller. On her eighth birthday, she had grown another 4 in. How tall was Anne on her eighth birthday? Write your answer in inches. 47 in

(8) Write these distances in feet.

6 yd — 18 ft
72 in — 6 ft
114 in — 9.5 ft

17

Your child should be familiar with smaller distances but may be unsure about the length of a mile. Go for a walk or a drive with your child and show him or her how you can use a pedometer or odometer to measure 1 mile.

Answers:

18–19 Length Problems 2

20–21 Perimeter Problems

18 19

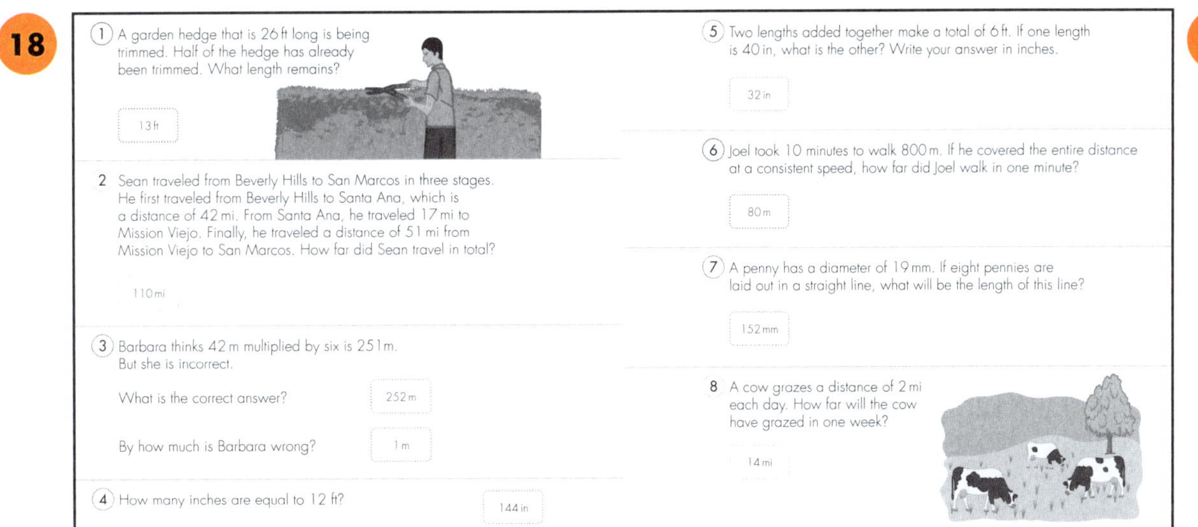

1 A garden hedge that is 26 ft long is being trimmed. Half of the hedge has already been trimmed. What length remains?

13 ft

2 Sean traveled from Beverly Hills to San Marcos in three stages. He first traveled from Beverly Hills to Santa Ana, which is a distance of 42 mi. From Santa Ana, he traveled 17 mi to Mission Viejo. Finally, he traveled a distance of 51 mi from Mission Viejo to San Marcos. How far did Sean travel in total?

110 mi

3 Barbara thinks 42 m multiplied by six is 251 m. But she is incorrect.

What is the correct answer? 252 m

By how much is Barbara wrong? 1 m

4 How many inches are equal to 12 ft? 144 in

5 Two lengths added together make a total of 6 ft. If one length is 40 in, what is the other? Write your answer in inches.

32 in

6 Joel took 10 minutes to walk 800 m. If he covered the entire distance at a consistent speed, how far did Joel walk in one minute?

80 m

7 A penny has a diameter of 19 mm. If eight pennies are laid out in a straight line, what will be the length of this line?

152 mm

8 A cow grazes a distance of 2 mi each day. How far will the cow have grazed in one week?

14 mi

When driving in a car with your child, you can take advantage of the opportunity to point out road signs that measure or list distances in miles. This will help him or her grasp the concept of distance.

20 21

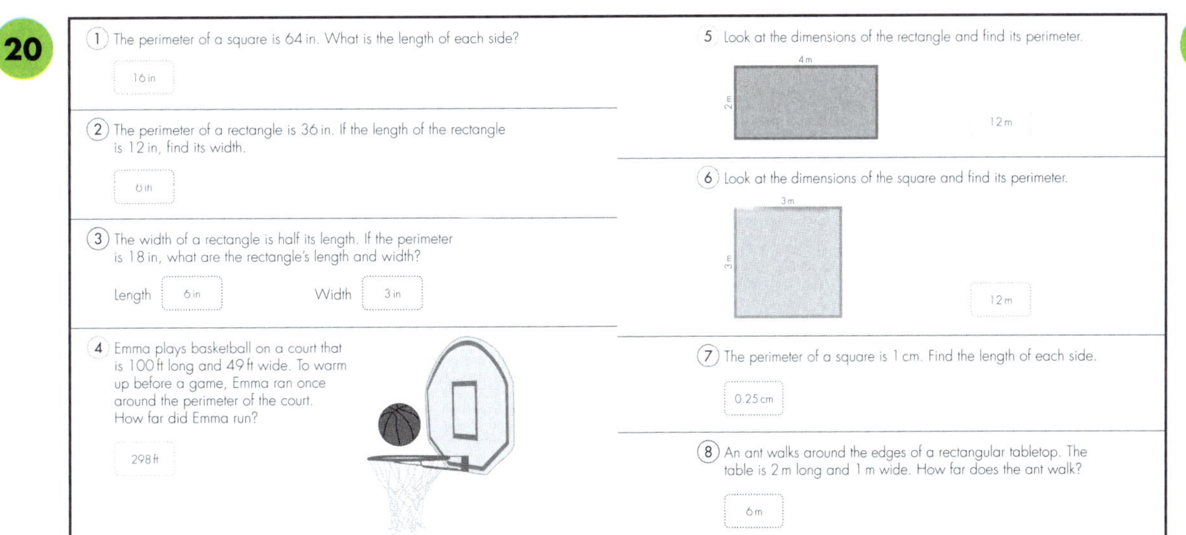

1 The perimeter of a square is 64 in. What is the length of each side?

16 in

2 The perimeter of a rectangle is 36 in. If the length of the rectangle is 12 in, find its width.

6 in

3 The width of a rectangle is half its length. If the perimeter is 18 in, what are the rectangle's length and width?

Length 6 in Width 3 in

4 Emma plays basketball on a court that is 100 ft long and 49 ft wide. To warm up before a game, Emma ran once around the perimeter of the court. How far did Emma run?

298 ft

5 Look at the dimensions of the rectangle and find its perimeter.

12 m

6 Look at the dimensions of the square and find its perimeter.

12 m

7 The perimeter of a square is 1 cm. Find the length of each side.

0.25 cm

8 An ant walks around the edges of a rectangular tabletop. The table is 2 m long and 1 m wide. How far does the ant walk?

6 m

Explain to your child that one of the reasons we measure perimeter is to estimate the length of a fence or wall we might build around an area of land. Encourage your child to first estimate and then measure the perimeter of his or her room at home.

Answers:

22–23 Perimeter and Length Problems
24–25 Areas of Squares and Rectangles 1

22

1) A washing machine and a dryer are each 26 in wide. What is their total width?

52 in

2) The distance between Akron and Barberton is 8 miles. If Peter cycled from Akron to Barberton and back again, how far did he cycle in total?

16 miles

3) The perimeter of a rectangle is 30 cm. If the longer side is 8 cm, what is the length of the shorter side?

7 cm

4) A rectangular parking lot is 70 yd long and 120 yd wide. What is the perimeter of the parking lot?

380 yd

23

5) A brick wall was 72 in high. A part of the wall was damaged in a storm. If the height of the wall is 48 in after the storm, how much height was lost?

24 in

6) Jack threw a ball a distance of 15 yd and Mary threw it a distance of 22 yd. How much farther did Mary throw the ball?

7 yd

7) Write these lengths in inches.

2 ft	3 ft	1 ft 6 in
24 in	36 in	18 in

8) The perimeter of a square is 36 in. What is the length of each side?

9 in

Your child needs to know how to convert between units such as inches and feet, and feet and yards. It is also helpful at this age if he or she can convert half units, such as one-and-a-half feet is the same as 18 inches.

24

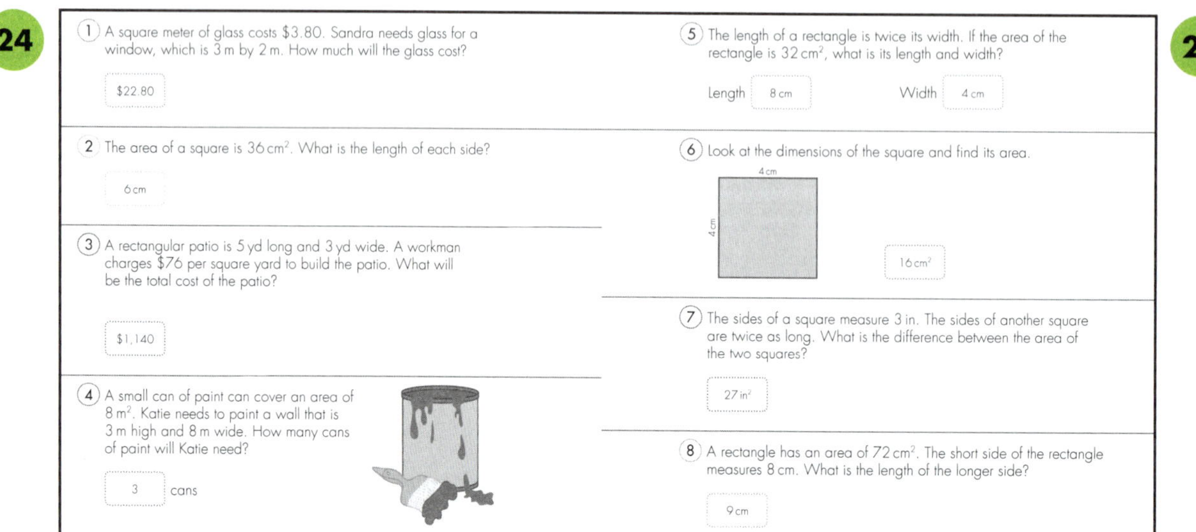

1) A square meter of glass costs \$3.80. Sandra needs glass for a window, which is 3 m by 2 m. How much will the glass cost?

\$22.80

2) The area of a square is 36 cm². What is the length of each side?

6 cm

3) A rectangular patio is 5 yd long and 3 yd wide. A workman charges \$76 per square yard to build the patio. What will be the total cost of the patio?

\$1,140

4) A small can of paint can cover an area of 8 m². Katie needs to paint a wall that is 3 m high and 8 m wide. How many cans of paint will Katie need?

3 cans

25

5) The length of a rectangle is twice its width. If the area of the rectangle is 32 cm², what is its length and width?

Length 8 cm Width 4 cm

6) Look at the dimensions of the square and find its area.

16 cm²

7) The sides of a square measure 3 in. The sides of another square are twice as long. What is the difference between the area of the two squares?

27 in²

8) A rectangle has an area of 72 cm². The short side of the rectangle measures 8 cm. What is the length of the longer side?

9 cm

Your child must understand that area means the amount of space inside a shape and is always measured in square units, such as square inches and square feet. Remind your child to always make sure the correct units have been written after the number.

Answers:

26–27 Areas of Squares and Rectangles 2

28–29 Areas of Compound Shapes

26

1 Karen's parents want to lay a new carpet in her bedroom. The bedroom floor is 4 m long and 3 m wide.

What area of new carpet is required? 12 m²

If the carpet costs $10 per square meter, how much will Karen's new bedroom carpet cost? $120

2 A builder draws the rectangular shape of a house he plans to build on graph paper. Look at his drawing below and the scale, and then calculate the area of the proposed house.

Area of house

Scale
1 grid square = 1 m²

Area of house 120 m²

3 A parking space in a garage is 4 m long and 2 m wide. What is the area of the parking space? 8 m²

4 A square has an area of 144 cm². What is the length of each side? 12 cm

27

5 The area of a rectangle is 72 ft². If the width of the rectangle is 4 ft, then what is its length? 18 ft

6 The width of a TV screen is 24 in and the height is 14 in. What is the area of the screen? 336 in²

7 The area of a rectangle is 50 in². The length of the rectangle is two times its width. Calculate the length and the width of the rectangle.

Length 10 in Width 5 in

8 A table is placed in the center of a carpet that has an area of 9 ft². If the table has an area of 2 ft², what is the area of the carpet around the table? 7 ft²

Even though the questions on this page involve only the areas of squares and rectangles, broaden your child's understanding of area to cover other shapes, such as circles. Point out coins, plates, or pizzas as examples of circular areas.

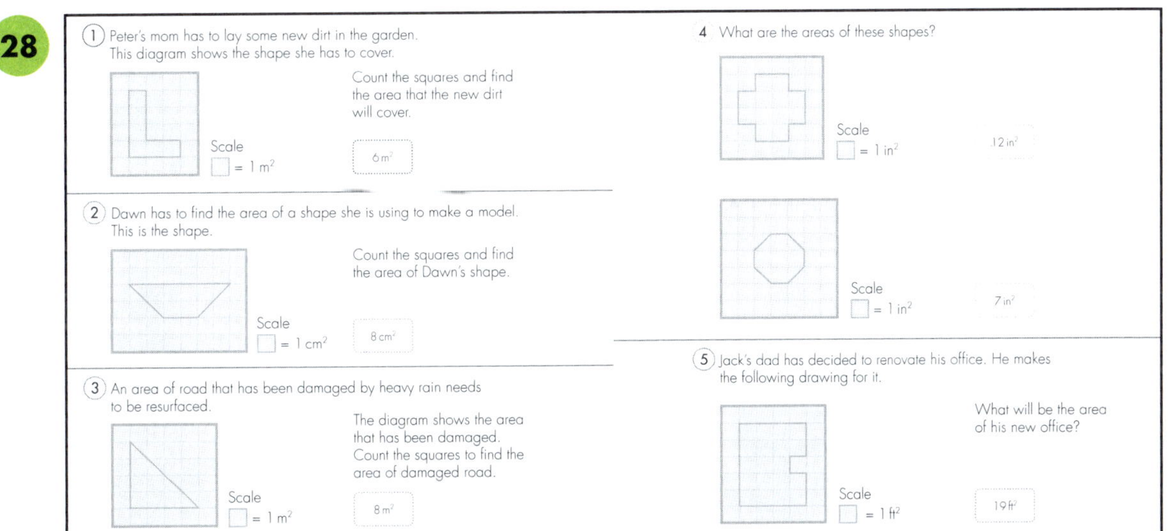

28

1 Peter's mom has to lay some new dirt in the garden. This diagram shows the shape she has to cover.

Count the squares and find the area that the new dirt will cover.

Scale
□ = 1 m²

6 m²

2 Dawn has to find the area of a shape she is using to make a model. This is the shape.

Count the squares and find the area of Dawn's shape.

Scale
□ = 1 cm²

8 cm²

3 An area of road that has been damaged by heavy rain needs to be resurfaced.

The diagram shows the area that has been damaged. Count the squares to find the area of damaged road.

Scale
□ = 1 m²

8 m²

29

4 What are the areas of these shapes?

Scale
□ = 1 in²

12 in²

Scale
□ = 1 in²

7 in²

5 Jack's dad has decided to renovate his office. He makes the following drawing for it.

What will be the area of his new office?

Scale
□ = 1 ft²

19 ft²

Although most of the compound shapes in these questions are fairly simple, some of the drawings contain halves of squares. Your child must carefully count all of them. Marking on the diagrams whether they are halves or wholes may also be helpful when determining area.

Answers:

30–31 Weights and Measures 1
32–33 Weights and Measures 2

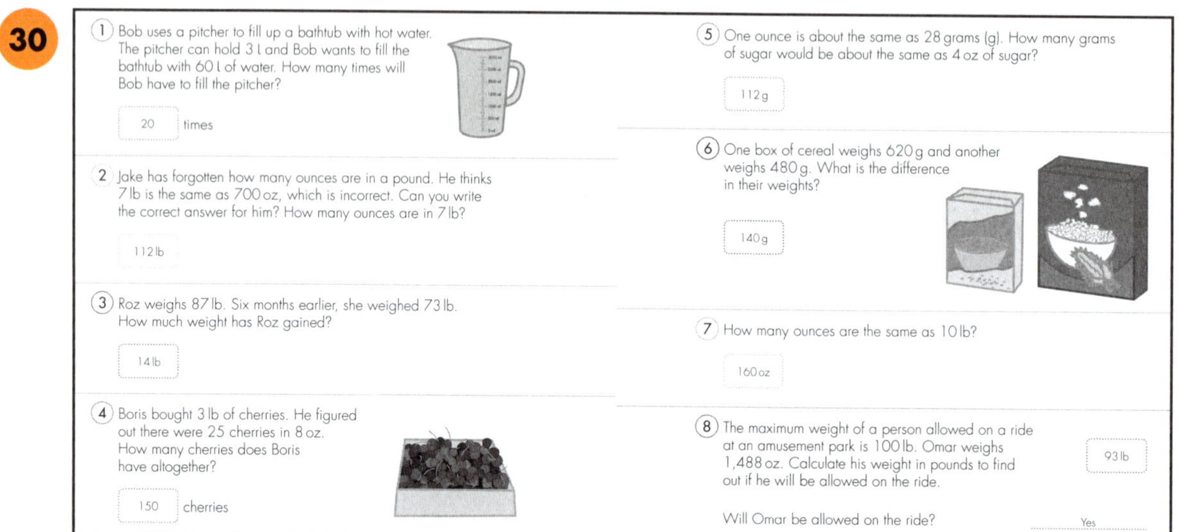

30

1. Bob uses a pitcher to fill up a bathtub with hot water. The pitcher can hold 3 l and Bob wants to fill the bathtub with 60 l of water. How many times will Bob have to fill the pitcher?

   20 times

2. Jake has forgotten how many ounces are in a pound. He thinks 7 lb is the same as 700 oz, which is incorrect. Can you write the correct answer for him? How many ounces are in 7 lb?

   112 lb

3. Roz weighs 87 lb. Six months earlier, she weighed 73 lb. How much weight has Roz gained?

   14 lb

4. Boris bought 3 lb of cherries. He figured out there were 25 cherries in 8 oz. How many cherries does Boris have altogether?

   150 cherries

31

5. One ounce is about the same as 28 grams (g). How many grams of sugar would be about the same as 4 oz of sugar?

   112 g

6. One box of cereal weighs 620 g and another weighs 480 g. What is the difference in their weights?

   140 g

7. How many ounces are the same as 10 lb?

   160 oz

8. The maximum weight of a person allowed on a ride at an amusement park is 100 lb. Omar weighs 1,488 oz. Calculate his weight in pounds to find out if he will be allowed on the ride.

   93 lb

   Will Omar be allowed on the ride? Yes

Imagining the scenario described in a problem is the key to solving the problem. If your child finds that difficult, try to relate the problem in some way to items or situations at home.

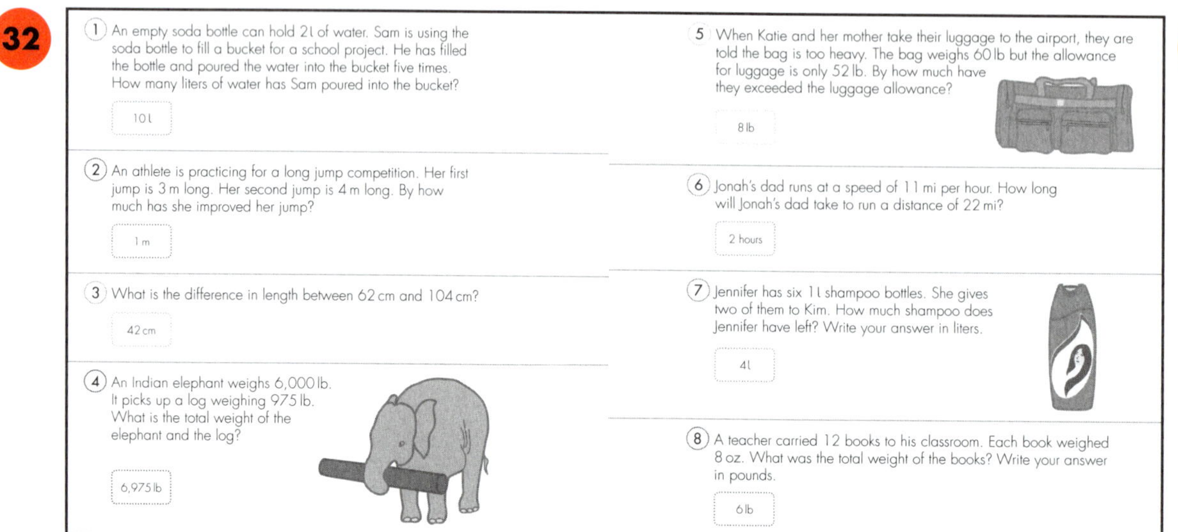

32

1. An empty soda bottle can hold 2 l of water. Sam is using the soda bottle to fill a bucket for a school project. He has filled the bottle and poured the water into the bucket five times. How many liters of water has Sam poured into the bucket?

   10 l

2. An athlete is practicing for a long jump competition. Her first jump is 3 m long. Her second jump is 4 m long. By how much has she improved her jump?

   1 m

3. What is the difference in length between 62 cm and 104 cm?

   42 cm

4. An Indian elephant weighs 6,000 lb. It picks up a log weighing 975 lb. What is the total weight of the elephant and the log?

   6,975 lb

33

5. When Katie and her mother take their luggage to the airport, they are told the bag is too heavy. The bag weighs 60 lb but the allowance for luggage is only 52 lb. By how much have they exceeded the luggage allowance?

   8 lb

6. Jonah's dad runs at a speed of 11 mi per hour. How long will Jonah's dad take to run a distance of 22 mi?

   2 hours

7. Jennifer has six 1 l shampoo bottles. She gives two of them to Kim. How much shampoo does Jennifer have left? Write your answer in liters.

   4 l

8. A teacher carried 12 books to his classroom. Each book weighed 8 oz. What was the total weight of the books? Write your answer in pounds.

   6 lb

Young children are likely to be familiar with smaller amounts such as pounds and ounces. Introduce your child slowly to working with larger amounts, such as tons, and metric amounts, such as liters and kilograms, so he or she can gradually build confidence using them.

Answers:

34–35 Measurement Problems

36–37 Money Problems 2, see p.80

38–39 Understanding Graphs 1

34 35

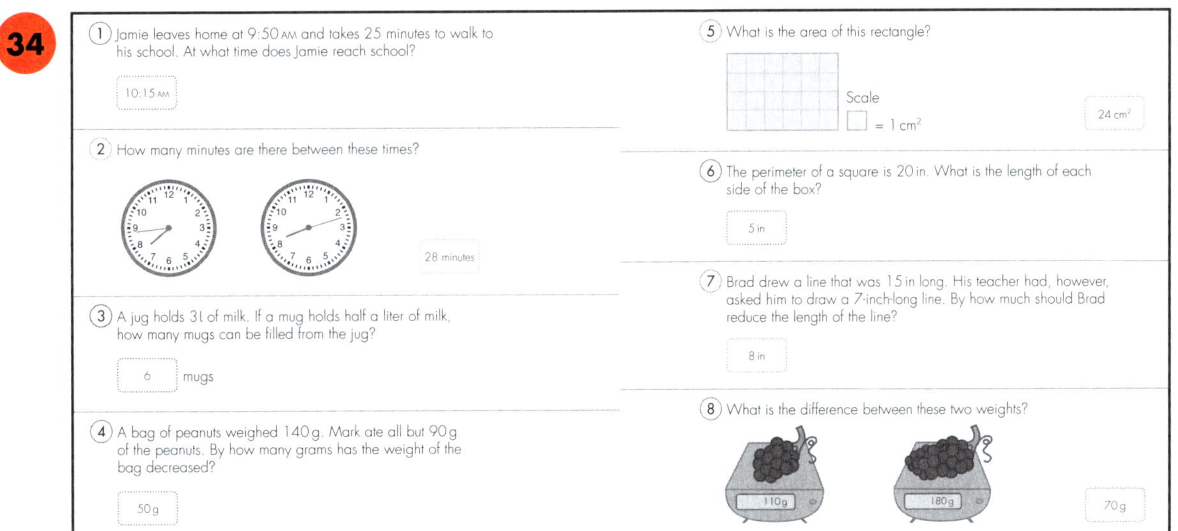

1. Jamie leaves home at 9:50 AM and takes 25 minutes to walk to his school. At what time does Jamie reach school?

   10:15 AM

2. How many minutes are there between these times?

   28 minutes

3. A jug holds 3 l of milk. If a mug holds half a liter of milk, how many mugs can be filled from the jug?

   6 mugs

4. A bag of peanuts weighed 140 g. Mark ate all but 90 g of the peanuts. By how many grams has the weight of the bag decreased?

   50 g

5. What is the area of this rectangle?

   Scale □ = 1 cm²

   24 cm²

6. The perimeter of a square is 20 in. What is the length of each side of the box?

   5 in

7. Brad drew a line that was 15 in long. His teacher had, however, asked him to draw a 7-inch-long line. By how much should Brad reduce the length of the line?

   8 in

8. What is the difference between these two weights?

   110 g 180 g

   70 g

Make sure your child is familiar with and comfortable using all the correct abbreviations for all of the main units, including both imperial units and metric units.

38 39

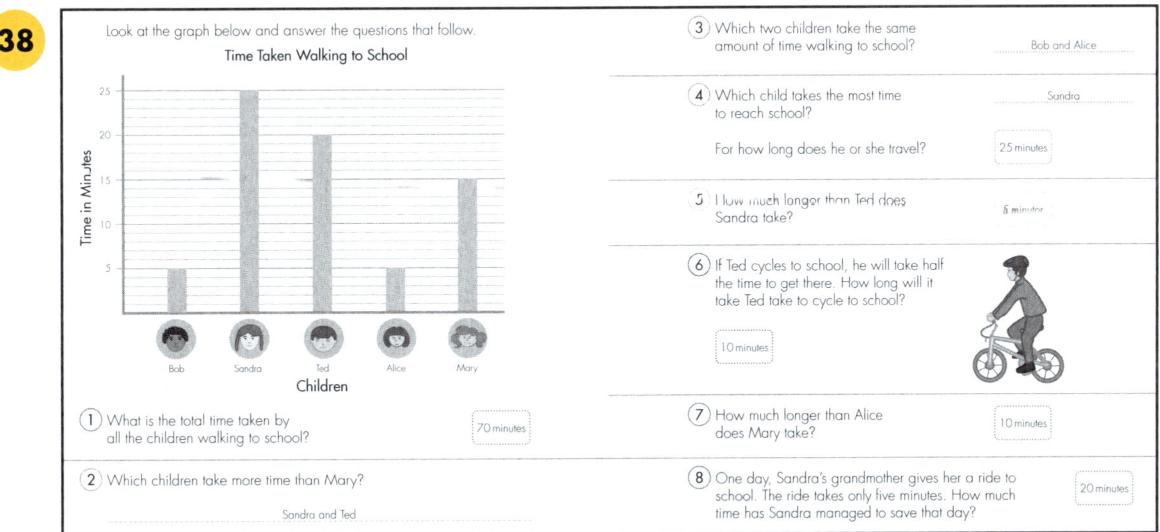

Look at the graph below and answer the questions that follow.

Time Taken Walking to School

1. What is the total time taken by all the children walking to school?

   70 minutes

2. Which children take more time than Mary?

   Sandra and Ted

3. Which two children take the same amount of time walking to school?

   Bob and Alice

4. Which child takes the most time to reach school?

   Sandra

   For how long does he or she travel?

   25 minutes

5. How much longer than Ted does Sandra take?

   5 minutes

6. If Ted cycles to school, he will take half the time to get there. How long will it take Ted take to cycle to school?

   10 minutes

7. How much longer than Alice does Mary take?

   10 minutes

8. One day, Sandra's grandmother gives her a ride to school. The ride takes only five minutes. How much time has Sandra managed to save that day?

   20 minutes

Encourage your child to look at information displays such as sports scoreboards and music charts. Ask questions based on the information to see if he or she can read the data correctly.

Answers:

40–41 Understanding Graphs 2
42–43 Addition and Subtraction 1

40

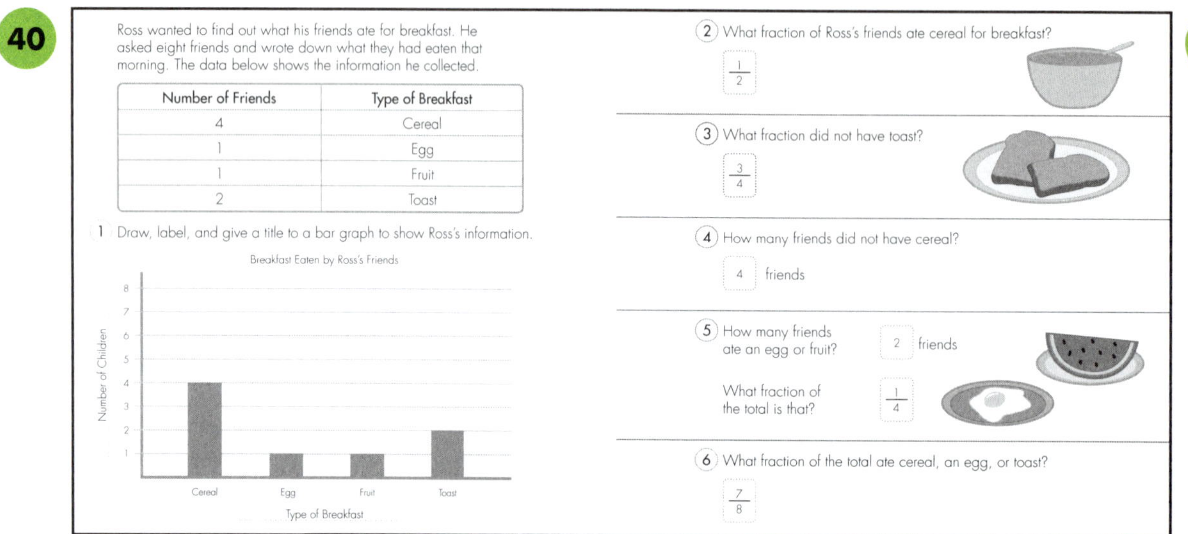

41

Encourage your child to make his or her own picture graphs based on data he or she has collected. For example, your child could ask 10 of his or her friends what fruit they like to eat most, and then plot the collected data on a graph.

42

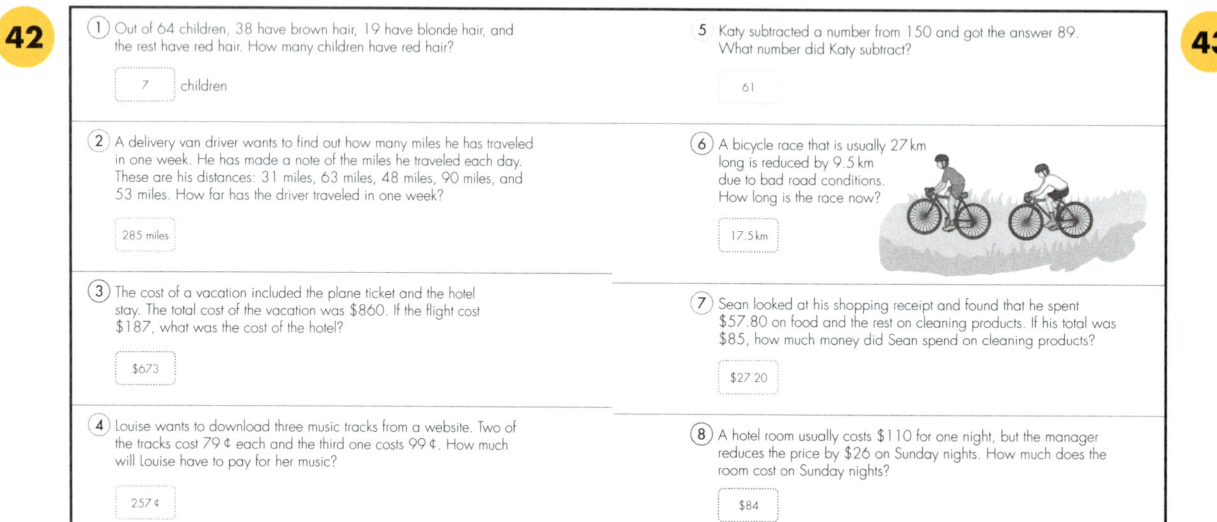

43

Your child needs to understand that addition is about combining groups or sets of items, and that many different words may be used to describe that process. Ensure your child is familiar with synonyms for "add," such as "combine," "put together," and "join."

Answers:

44–45 Addition and Subtraction 2

46–47 Addition and Subtraction 3

44

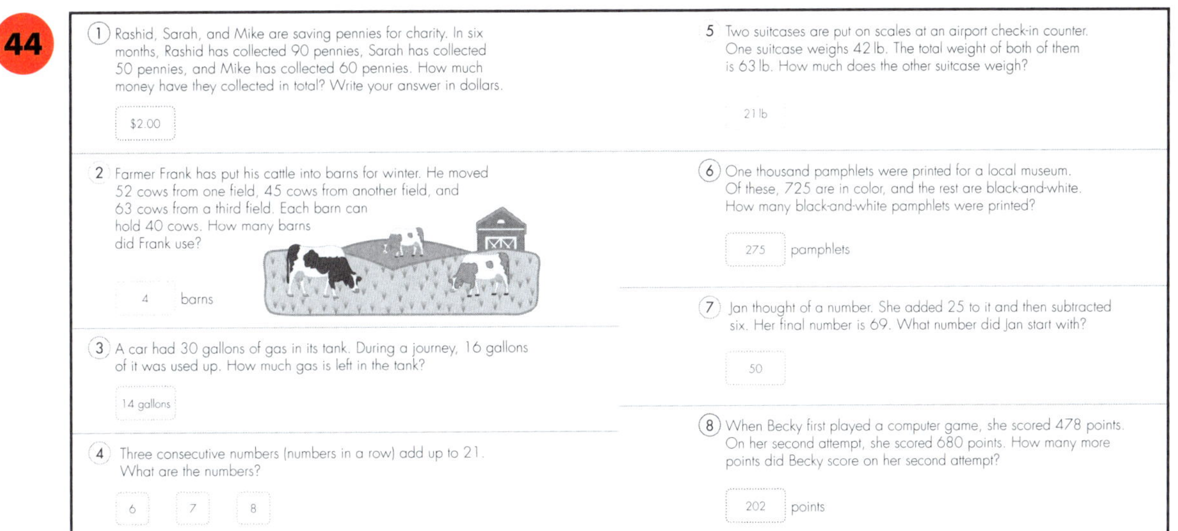

1. Rashid, Sarah, and Mike are saving pennies for charity. In six months, Rashid has collected 90 pennies, Sarah has collected 50 pennies, and Mike has collected 60 pennies. How much money have they collected in total? Write your answer in dollars.

   $2.00

2. Farmer Frank has put his cattle into barns for winter. He moved 52 cows from one field, 45 cows from another field, and 63 cows from a third field. Each barn can hold 40 cows. How many barns did Frank use?

   4 barns

3. A car had 30 gallons of gas in its tank. During a journey, 16 gallons of it was used up. How much gas is left in the tank?

   14 gallons

4. Three consecutive numbers (numbers in a row) add up to 21. What are the numbers?

   6 7 8

45

5. Two suitcases are put on scales at an airport check-in counter. One suitcase weighs 42 lb. The total weight of both of them is 63 lb. How much does the other suitcase weigh?

   21 lb

6. One thousand pamphlets were printed for a local museum. Of these, 725 are in color, and the rest are black-and-white. How many black-and-white pamphlets were printed?

   275 pamphlets

7. Jan thought of a number. She added 25 to it and then subtracted six. Her final number is 69. What number did Jan start with?

   50

8. When Becky first played a computer game, she scored 478 points. On her second attempt, she scored 680 points. How many more points did Becky score on her second attempt?

   202 points

It is possible your child has been taught different methods of addition and subtraction. Make sure you understand how he or she is solving the problems. If you are not sure, ask your child or the teacher.

46

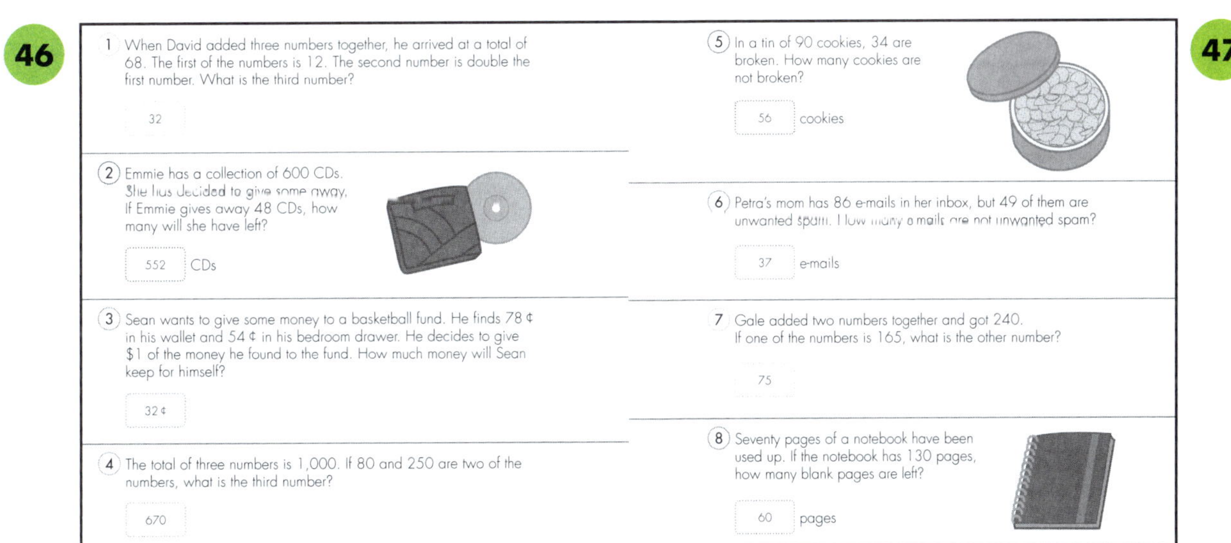

1. When David added three numbers together, he arrived at a total of 68. The first of the numbers is 12. The second number is double the first number. What is the third number?

   32

2. Emmie has a collection of 600 CDs. She has decided to give some away. If Emmie gives away 48 CDs, how many will she have left?

   552 CDs

3. Sean wants to give some money to a basketball fund. He finds 78 ¢ in his wallet and 54 ¢ in his bedroom drawer. He decides to give $1 of the money he found to the fund. How much money will Sean keep for himself?

   32 ¢

4. The total of three numbers is 1,000. If 80 and 250 are two of the numbers, what is the third number?

   670

47

5. In a tin of 90 cookies, 34 are broken. How many cookies are not broken?

   56 cookies

6. Petra's mom has 86 e-mails in her inbox, but 49 of them are unwanted spam. How many e-mails are not unwanted spam?

   37 e-mails

7. Gale added two numbers together and got 240. If one of the numbers is 165, what is the other number?

   75

8. Seventy pages of a notebook have been used up. If the notebook has 130 pages, how many blank pages are left?

   60 pages

Your child should have a good working knowledge of addition and subtraction before he or she moves on to learning times tables and multiplication.

Answers:

48–49 Multiplication and Division 1
50–51 Multiplication and Division 2

48

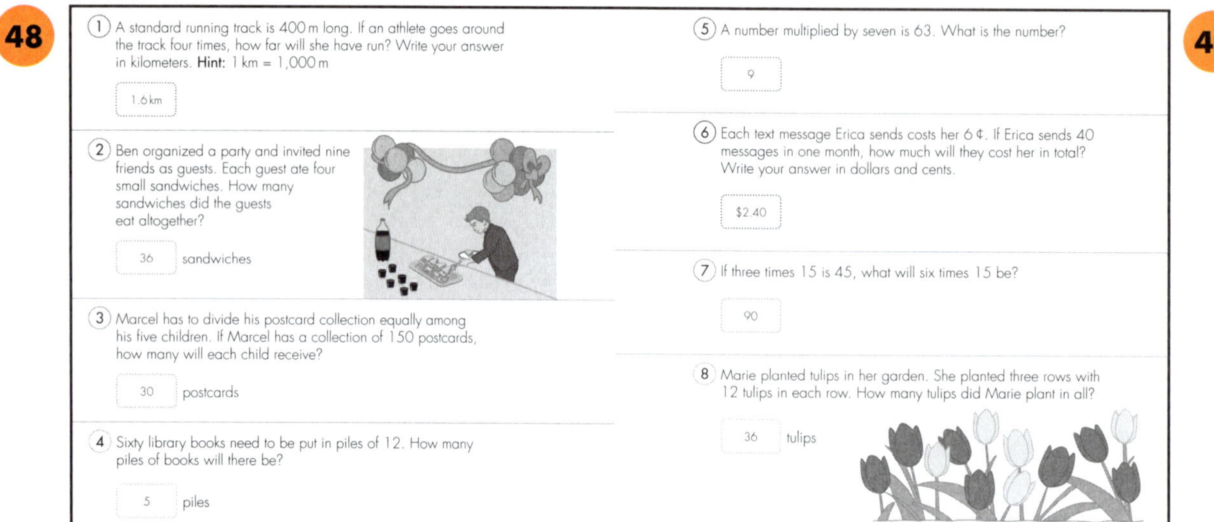
1) A standard running track is 400 m long. If an athlete goes around the track four times, how far will she have run? Write your answer in kilometers. **Hint:** 1 km = 1,000 m

1.6 km

2) Ben organized a party and invited nine friends as guests. Each guest ate four small sandwiches. How many sandwiches did the guests eat altogether?

36 sandwiches

3) Marcel has to divide his postcard collection equally among his five children. If Marcel has a collection of 150 postcards, how many will each child receive?

30 postcards

4) Sixty library books need to be put in piles of 12. How many piles of books will there be?

5 piles

5) A number multiplied by seven is 63. What is the number?

9

6) Each text message Erica sends costs her 6¢. If Erica sends 40 messages in one month, how much will they cost her in total? Write your answer in dollars and cents.

$2.40

7) If three times 15 is 45, what will six times 15 be?

90

8) Marie planted tulips in her garden. She planted three rows with 12 tulips in each row. How many tulips did Marie plant in all?

36 tulips

49

It is tempting for children and parents to think of multiplication and division as two different things, but they are closely related. They are called "inverse" of each other. If a child knows 3 x 4 is 12, they also know 12 ÷ 3 is 4 and 12 ÷ 4 is 3.

50

1) In a video game, a player is awarded 15 points every time the frog catches a fly, and 20 points when the frog catches a wasp. How many points will a player earn if the frog catches six flies and nine wasps?

270 points

2) Charlie has saved 50¢ every day for 21 days. How much money has Charlie saved in total? Write your answer in dollars and cents.

$10.50

3) A teacher graded 64 test booklets every evening for six days. How many booklets did the teacher grade in total?

384 booklets

4) Pat went to the gym 132 times in a year. If she went an equal number of times each month, how many gym visits did she make each month?

11 times

5) A parcel delivery company has 520 parcels to be delivered by four drivers. How many parcels will each driver need to deliver?

130 parcels

6) Victor thinks of a number that is seven times smaller than 56. Which number is he thinking of?

8

7) Debbie multiplied a number by itself and got 81 as the product. Which number did Debbie start with?

9

8) A birthday cake is covered with chocolate candies and cut into eight pieces. Each piece has 6 candies except one piece, which has 7. How many chocolate candies were put on the cake?

49 candies

51

Knowing the times tables is the key to solving the problems on these pages. Your child should work on learning the tables up to 12 x 12 and also be aware of multiples of 15 and 20.

Answers:

52–53 Multiplication and Division 3

54–55 Money Problems 3, see p.80

56–57 Times Tables Problems 1

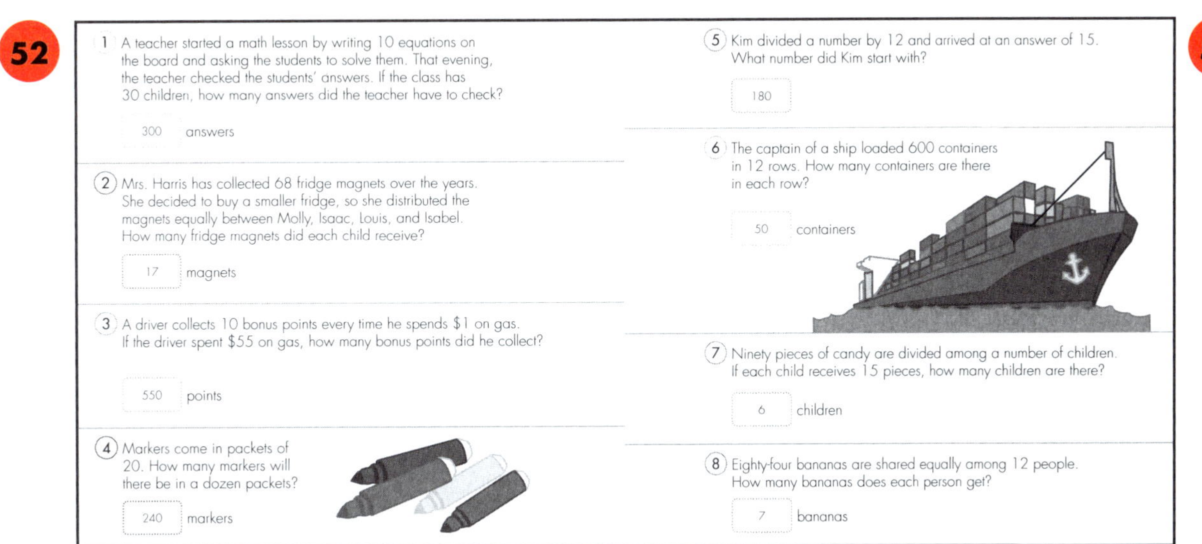

52

1 A teacher started a math lesson by writing 10 equations on the board and asking the students to solve them. That evening, the teacher checked the students' answers. If the class has 30 children, how many answers did the teacher have to check?

300 answers

2 Mrs. Harris has collected 68 fridge magnets over the years. She decided to buy a smaller fridge, so she distributed the magnets equally between Molly, Isaac, Louis, and Isabel. How many fridge magnets did each child receive?

17 magnets

3 A driver collects 10 bonus points every time he spends $1 on gas. If the driver spent $55 on gas, how many bonus points did he collect?

550 points

4 Markers come in packets of 20. How many markers will there be in a dozen packets?

240 markers

53

5 Kim divided a number by 12 and arrived at an answer of 15. What number did Kim start with?

180

6 The captain of a ship loaded 600 containers in 12 rows. How many containers are there in each row?

50 containers

7 Ninety pieces of candy are divided among a number of children. If each child receives 15 pieces, how many children are there?

6 children

8 Eighty-four bananas are shared equally among 12 people. How many bananas does each person get?

7 bananas

Children can sometimes have difficulty understanding the direct relationship between multiplication and division. Always encourage your child to connect the two when solving equations.

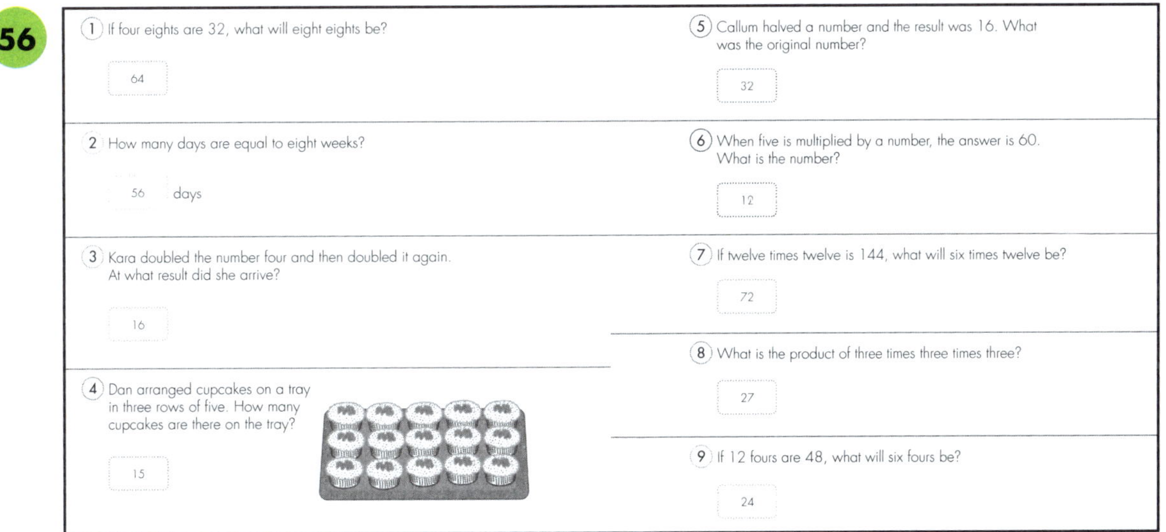

56

1 If four eights are 32, what will eight eights be?

64

2 How many days are equal to eight weeks?

56 days

3 Kara doubled the number four and then doubled it again. At what result did she arrive?

16

4 Dan arranged cupcakes on a tray in three rows of five. How many cupcakes are there on the tray?

15

57

5 Callum halved a number and the result was 16. What was the original number?

32

6 When five is multiplied by a number, the answer is 60. What is the number?

12

7 If twelve times twelve is 144, what will six times twelve be?

72

8 What is the product of three times three times three?

27

9 If 12 fours are 48, what will six fours be?

24

Help your child discover that when practicing a particular times table, he or she actually learns two! For example, if your child learns 3 x 5 is 15, he or she also knows 5 x 3 is 15.

Answers:

58–59 Times Tables Problems 2

60–61 Times Tables Problems 3

58

1. Billy is 7 years old, and Mandy is 12 years old. How many months old are they?

   Billy is 84 months old. Mandy is 144 months old.

2. A boy earns $15 per day shoveling snow in the winter.

   If he works five days a week, how much will he earn? $75

   If he works seven days a week and gets an extra $2 for each day of weekend work, how much will he earn? $109

3. It costs Jill $12 each time she has a piano lesson. If Jill has nine lessons, how much will they cost her in total?

   $108

   In the summer, the cost of each piano lesson drops. If Jill has eight summer lessons and they cost her a total of $72, how much does each lesson cost?

   $9

59

4. For a party, five children collect eight pairs of sunglasses each. How many pairs of sunglasses do they have altogether?

   40 pairs of sunglasses

5. How many days are there in nine weeks?

   63 days

6. Seven children have collected eight party hats each. What is the total number of hats they have for the party?

   56 hats

7. How many months are there in five years?

   60 months

8. A teacher has drawn six octagons on the board. How many sides has he drawn in total?

   48 sides

The 7 and 8 times tables are often considered to be the most difficult to remember. Spend time helping your child learn these times tables thoroughly—especially at the higher combinations, such as 6 x 7 and 8 x 9.

60

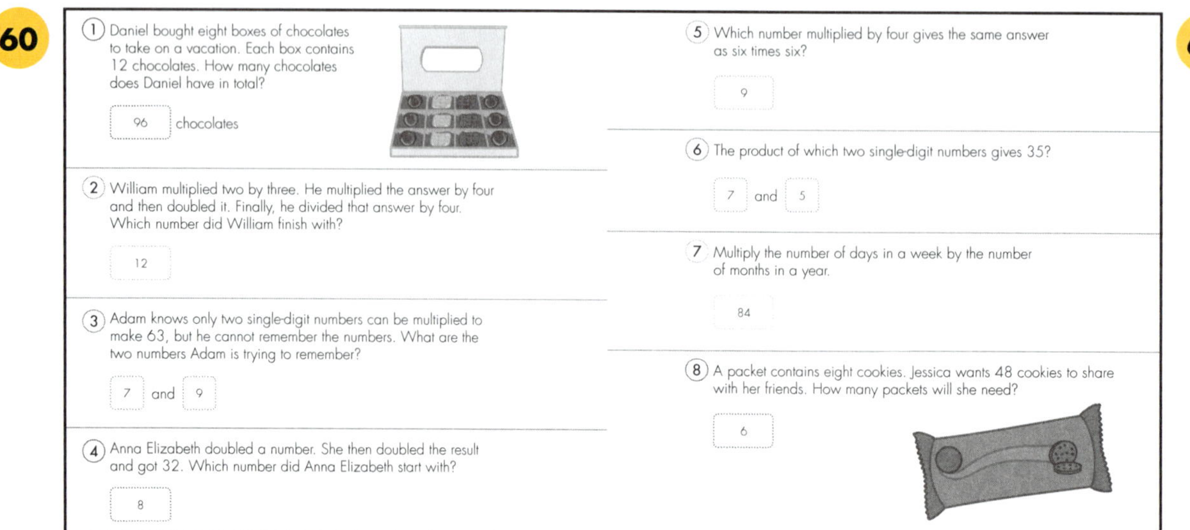

1. Daniel bought eight boxes of chocolates to take on a vacation. Each box contains 12 chocolates. How many chocolates does Daniel have in total?

   96 chocolates

2. William multiplied two by three. He multiplied the answer by four and then doubled it. Finally, he divided that answer by four. Which number did William finish with?

   12

3. Adam knows only two single-digit numbers can be multiplied to make 63, but he cannot remember the numbers. What are the two numbers Adam is trying to remember?

   7 and 9

4. Anna Elizabeth doubled a number. She then doubled the result and got 32. Which number did Anna Elizabeth start with?

   8

5. Which number multiplied by four gives the same answer as six times six?

   9

6. The product of which two single-digit numbers gives 35?

   7 and 5

7. Multiply the number of days in a week by the number of months in a year.

   84

8. A packet contains eight cookies. Jessica wants 48 cookies to share with her friends. How many packets will she need?

   6

61

When your child is consistently getting his or her times tables correct, concentrate on faster recall. You could generate some more interest by making it competitive, using a stopwatch or timer.

Answers:

62–63 Harder Problems 1

64–65 Harder Problems 2

62

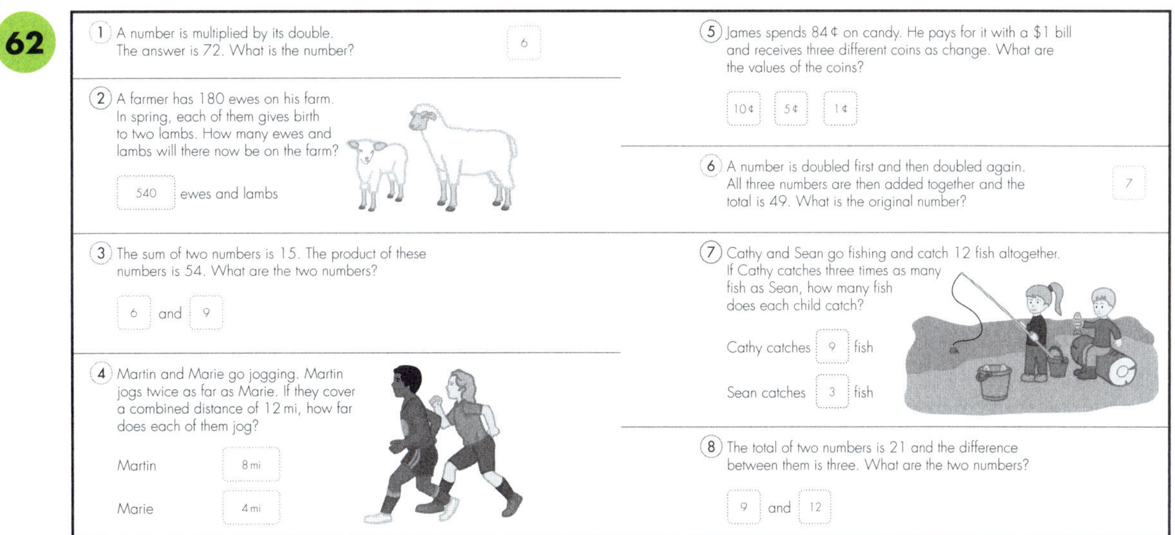

1. A number is multiplied by its double. The answer is 72. What is the number? 6
2. A farmer has 180 ewes on his farm. In spring, each of them gives birth to two lambs. How many ewes and lambs will there now be on the farm? 540 ewes and lambs
3. The sum of two numbers is 15. The product of these numbers is 54. What are the two numbers? 6 and 9
4. Martin and Marie go jogging. Martin jogs twice as far as Marie. If they cover a combined distance of 12 mi, how far does each of them jog?
   Martin 8 mi
   Marie 4 mi
5. James spends 84¢ on candy. He pays for it with a $1 bill and receives three different coins as change. What are the values of the coins? 10¢ 5¢ 1¢
6. A number is doubled first and then doubled again. All three numbers are then added together and the total is 49. What is the original number? 7
7. Cathy and Sean go fishing and catch 12 fish altogether. If Cathy catches three times as many fish as Sean, how many fish does each child catch?
   Cathy catches 9 fish
   Sean catches 3 fish
8. The total of two numbers is 21 and the difference between them is three. What are the two numbers? 9 and 12

63

Whatever the problem may be, it is always worth reading the question at least twice. If your child is in a hurry, he or she may miss something important or miss reading one of the numbers needed for the calculation.

64

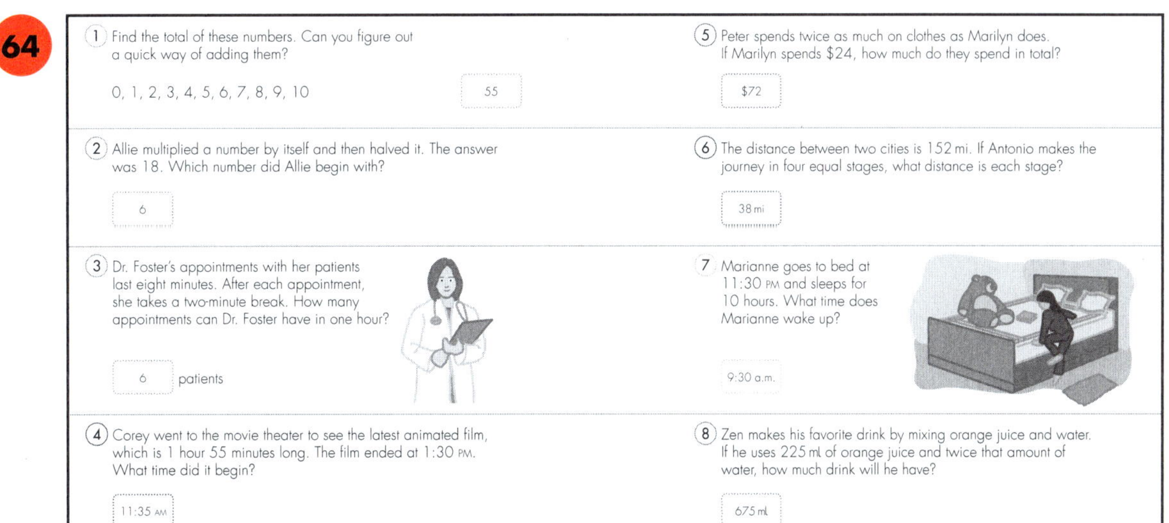

1. Find the total of these numbers. Can you figure out a quick way of adding them?
   0, 1, 2, 3, 4, 5, 6, 7, 8, 9, 10 55
2. Allie multiplied a number by itself and then halved it. The answer was 18. Which number did Allie begin with? 6
3. Dr. Foster's appointments with her patients last eight minutes. After each appointment, she takes a two-minute break. How many appointments can Dr. Foster have in one hour? 6 patients
4. Corey went to the movie theater to see the latest animated film, which is 1 hour 55 minutes long. The film ended at 1:30 PM. What time did it begin? 11:35 AM
5. Peter spends twice as much on clothes as Marilyn does. If Marilyn spends $24, how much do they spend in total? $72
6. The distance between two cities is 152 mi. If Antonio makes the journey in four equal stages, what distance is each stage? 38 mi
7. Marianne goes to bed at 11:30 PM and sleeps for 10 hours. What time does Marianne wake up? 9:30 a.m.
8. Zen makes his favorite drink by mixing orange juice and water. If he uses 225 ml of orange juice and twice that amount of water, how much drink will he have? 675 ml

65

The quick way to add consecutive numbers (0–10) is to multiply the number of consecutive numbers (11) by the middle number (5). Encourage your child to try this way. Once your child has solved a problem, ask him or her to read the question once more and check that the answer makes sense.

Answers:

14–15 Money Problems 1
36–37 Money Problems 2
54–55 Money Problems 3

These pages test your child's ability to solve problems involving amounts of money. Explain to your child the relationship between dollars and cents, and help him or her convert between these units quickly and easily. At this age, your child may have begun to experience spending money in stores. Stress the importance of knowing the cost of each item being bought, the amount of money handed over, and the amount of change he or she should receive.

14

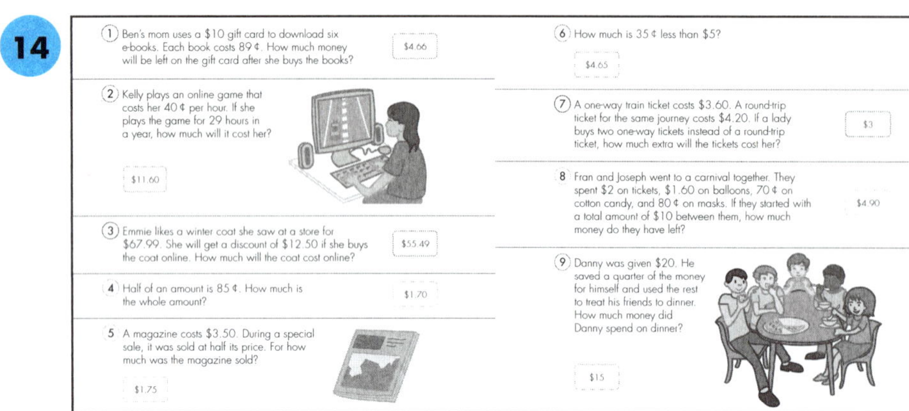

1. Ben's mom uses a $10 gift card to download six e-books. Each book costs 89¢. How much money will be left on the gift card after she buys the books? $4.66
2. Kelly plays an online game that costs her 40¢ per hour. If she plays the game for 29 hours in a year, how much will it cost her? $11.60
3. Emmie likes a winter coat she saw at a store for $67.99. She will get a discount of $12.50 if she buys the coat online. How much will the coat cost online? $55.49
4. Half of an amount is 85¢. How much is the whole amount? $1.70
5. A magazine costs $3.50. During a special sale, it was sold at half its price. For how much was the magazine sold? $1.75

15

6. How much is 35¢ less than $5? $4.65
7. A one-way train ticket costs $3.60. A round-trip ticket for the same journey costs $4.20. If a lady buys two one-way tickets instead of a round-trip ticket, how much extra will the tickets cost her? $3
8. Fran and Joseph went to a carnival together. They spent $2 on tickets, $1.60 on balloons, 70¢ on cotton candy, and 80¢ on masks. If they started with a total amount of $10 between them, how much money do they have left? $4.90
9. Danny was given $20. He saved a quarter of the money for himself and used the rest to treat his friends to dinner. How much money did Danny spend on dinner? $15

36

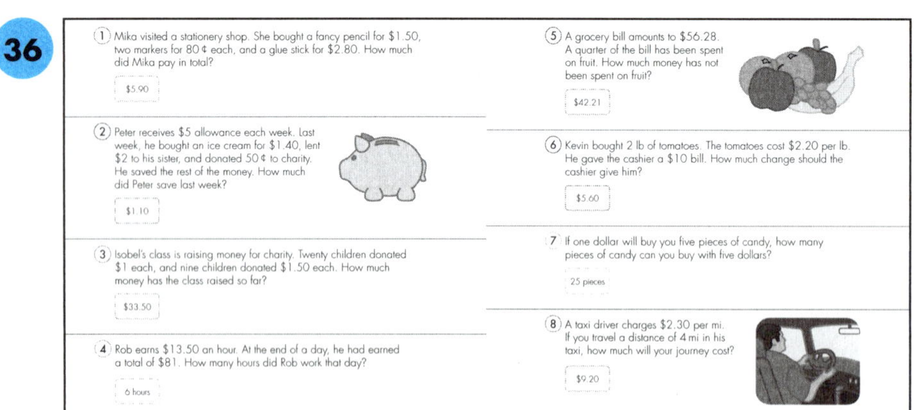

1. Mika visited a stationery shop. She bought a fancy pencil for $1.50, two markers for 80¢ each, and a glue stick for $2.80. How much did Mika pay in total? $5.90
2. Peter receives $5 allowance each week. Last week, he bought an ice cream for $1.40, lent $2 to his sister, and donated 50¢ to charity. He saved the rest of the money. How much did Peter save last week? $1.10
3. Isobel's class is raising money for charity. Twenty children donated $1 each, and nine children donated $1.50 each. How much money has the class raised so far? $33.50
4. Rob earns $13.50 an hour. At the end of a day, he had earned a total of $81. How many hours did Rob work that day? 6 hours

37

5. A grocery bill amounts to $56.28. A quarter of the bill has been spent on fruit. How much money has not been spent on fruit? $42.21
6. Kevin bought 2 lb of tomatoes. The tomatoes cost $2.20 per lb. He gave the cashier a $10 bill. How much change should the cashier give him? $5.60
7. If one dollar will buy you five pieces of candy, how many pieces of candy can you buy with five dollars? 25 pieces
8. A taxi driver charges $2.30 per mi. If you travel a distance of 4 mi in his taxi, how much will your journey cost? $9.20

54

1. Convert these amounts of money from cents to dollars.

1,000¢	$10	700¢	$7
250¢	$2.50	100¢	$1

2. $4 was shared equally among 5 children. How much money did each child receive? 80¢
3. William and Kate added their money together and then shared it equally among themselves and their son, George. If William had $3.50 and Kate had $5.50, how much money did George receive after the money was shared? $3
4. Claire, Bruno, Mark, and Ella went for lunch together. They shared the bill of $20.60 equally among themselves. How much money did each of them pay? $5.15

55

5. How many $5 bills make up $100? 20 bills
6. Sarah travels to work by bus. A round-trip ticket costs her $1.30 per day. If Sarah goes to work five days a week, how much does she spend on bus tickets each week? $6.50
7. Dan collected $3.60 for charity. His mom said she would give him twice the amount of money he collected.
   How much money will his mom give him? $7.20
   How much money would Dan have collected in total? $10.80
8. David got $200 as a birthday present. He bought himself two new video games that cost $49.99 each.
   How much did the two games cost in total? $99.98
   How much money does David have left after buying the two games? $100.02